Herbert Vivian

Tunisia and the modern Barbary Pirates

Herbert Vivian

Tunisia and the modern Barbary Pirates

ISBN/EAN: 9783743313897

Manufactured in Europe, USA, Canada, Australia, Japa

Cover: Foto ©ninafisch / pixelio.de

Manufactured and distributed by brebook publishing software (www.brebook.com)

Herbert Vivian

Tunisia and the modern Barbary Pirates

Contents

PREFACE . vii

Historical Introduction

The Berbers of Lybia—The Carthaginians (B.C. 1400-146)—A Roman Province (B.C. 146-A.D. 439)—The Vandals (A.D. 439-533)—The Byzantines (A.D. 533-698)—The Arabs (A.D. 698-1573)—The Beys A.D. 1573-1881) 1

Chapter I
THE BEY

The Prisoner of Marsa—A French Puppet—A State Prisoner—The Puppet's Shadow of State—Appearance—The Heir—A Modern Sovereign—The Palace at Marsa—The Bodyguard—The Gardens—The Menagery—The Palace at Tunis—The Bardo . 11

Chapter II
THE MODERN BARBARY PIRATES

French Administration—Finance—Taxes—Army—Unlike Algeria—Tunisia has an Astute Despotism—The Official Version Is highly coloured—Exactions of Official—A Great Gulf Fixed—Travel Hindered—Spy-Mania—Communications—Camp Followers, not Colonists—Vexatious Custom-Houses—The Future of the Country—Our Lost Opportunity . 27

Chapter III
THE CHILDREN OF THE MORNING

Arabs: (1) of Tunis and the Coast—Costume—Houses—(2) of the Interior—Types—Dwellings—Industries—Costume—(3) of the Oases—Costume—Dwellings—Industries—Troglodytes—Home Life—Harems—Vulgarizing by Civilization—Women's Rights—Marriage—Divorce—Funerals—Food—Water Drinking—Drugs—Of learning Arabic—Greetings—Curses—Proverbs . 41

CONTENTS

Chapter IV
ISLAM

Conversion to Islam — Mosques — Graveyards — Ramadan — Bairam — Drunken Moslems — Photography — The Aïssawas — Shrines and Seers — The Merabut of Baghdad — The Story of a Jinn — Amulets — Fortune-tellers 92

Chapter V
JEWS AND NIGGERS

The Jews of Tunis — "Leghorns" — Industries — Nomad Camp-followers — Education — Rapacity — Anti-Semitic Riots — Organization — Poor-Laws — Law-Giving — The Jewish Quarter — Houses — Religion — Ritual — Saints — Guardian Angels — The Sabbath — Missions to Jews — Food — The Family — A Wedding — A Funeral — Literature and Art — Negroes . 118

Chapter VI
IN AND OUT OF TUNIS

Arrival — First Impressions — Streets — Shops — A Street Story-teller — Snake-charmers — The French Quarter — Accommodation — Food — An Anglican Church — Beggars — Marsa — Carthage 144

Chapter VII
THE INSIDE OF THE CUP AND THE PLATTER

The Interior — Accommodation — Fonduks — Vermin — Fantasias — Art — Bicycles — An Itinerary — Tunis to Susa — Susa — Susa to Kairwân — Kairwân — Sabra — Susa to Sfax — El-Jem — Sfax — Fortifications — Gabes — A Sandstorm — Wells — Jerba — Sbeitla — Thala — El-Kef — Béja — The Mejerda — Dugga — Bizerta 184

Chapter VIII
TRADE AND AGRICULTURE

Vulture-Princes — Bazaars — Industries — Saddlery — Sheshias — Dyeing — Tanners — Carpets — Perfumes — Arms — Potteries — Halfa-Grass — Trade with the interior — Rhadames — Rhat — The Tuaregs — Agricultural Methods — Habbus — Wells — The Cactus — Vines — Olives — Fisheries — Sponges — Pulps 236

CONTENTS xiii

Chapter IX
JUSTICE AND EDUCATION

Justice—The Court of the Kadi—The Governor of Tunis—Public Executions—Prisons—The Right of Sanctuary—Capital Punishment—The Paradise of Criminals—Police Precautions—Modern Solomons—Education—Sadiki College—Alawi College . . 272

Chapter X
BEASTS AND FEATHERED FOWL

Camels—Locusts—Dogs—Flamingoes—Serpents—Scorpions—Gazelles 295

Chapter XI
TRIPOLI

The Town—The Outskirts—Security—Commerce—Palm-Wine—The Future of Tripoli 327

INDEX . 335

List of Illustrations

Roman Aqueduct near the Bardo
Square outside the Dar-el-Bey
Panorama from the Dar-el-Bey
Bardo Palace: Lion Staircase
A Man of Tunis
Gurbi: Doorway
Gurbi
Country Girl
Arab Countrywomen
Types of Women
Country Woman
Country Women
Woman of Oasis of Gabes
Middle-Class Woman and Servant
An Arab Funeral
After Blood-letting
Negro Bogey-Man dancing in Bairam
Jewish Dancing Girl
Boys in Best Clothes at Bairam
Bairam: Swings
A Fortune Teller
Gate of France, Tunis
Jewess
Tunis: A Street
Bab-Swika Square, Tunis
Tunis: A Door
Tunis: Snake Charmers
Street Cheese-Seller
Tunis: Avenue de France
Sisi bu Said
Carthage: Remains of the Basilica
Carthage: Old Cisterns of La Malga
Carthage: Restored Cisterns
Monks Excavating at Carthage
A Punic Tomb

	PAGE
Basilica at Carthage	181
A Fonduk	186
A Cook-Shop in Tunis	188
Arab Art	189
A Wayside Tavern	190
Susa	191
Susa: The Tramway Terminus for Kairwân	194
Kairwân	195
Kairwân: The Main Street	199
Kairwân: Interior of the Great Mosque	201
Kairwân: Mihrab of the Great Mosque	205
Kairwân Streets	207
Sabra	209
El-Jem Amphitheatre	210
Sfax: Market outside the Walls	212
Bread-Stall in the Oasis of Gabes	214
Oasis of Gabes: Interior of a House	215
Oasis of Gabes: Roman Barrage still used for irrigation	217
A Wayside Well between El-Jem and Sfax	220
Dugga: Corinthian Temple	228
Bizerta Ferry: Passage of a Funeral	233
Guard at the entrance of the Bazaars	240
Bazaars of Tunis	241
The Saddlers' Bazaar	245
Bazaars of Tunis	249
Bazaars of Tunis	251
A Carpet Weaver	253
The Perfume Bazaar	255
A Public Execution, 1	276
A Public Execution, 2	278
A Public Execution, 3	279
A Moslem School	288
Racing Camel	297
Camels drawing Water from a Well	301
Caravan Passing through an Oasis	305
A Camel Tent Open	307
Camel Cavalcade on the March	309

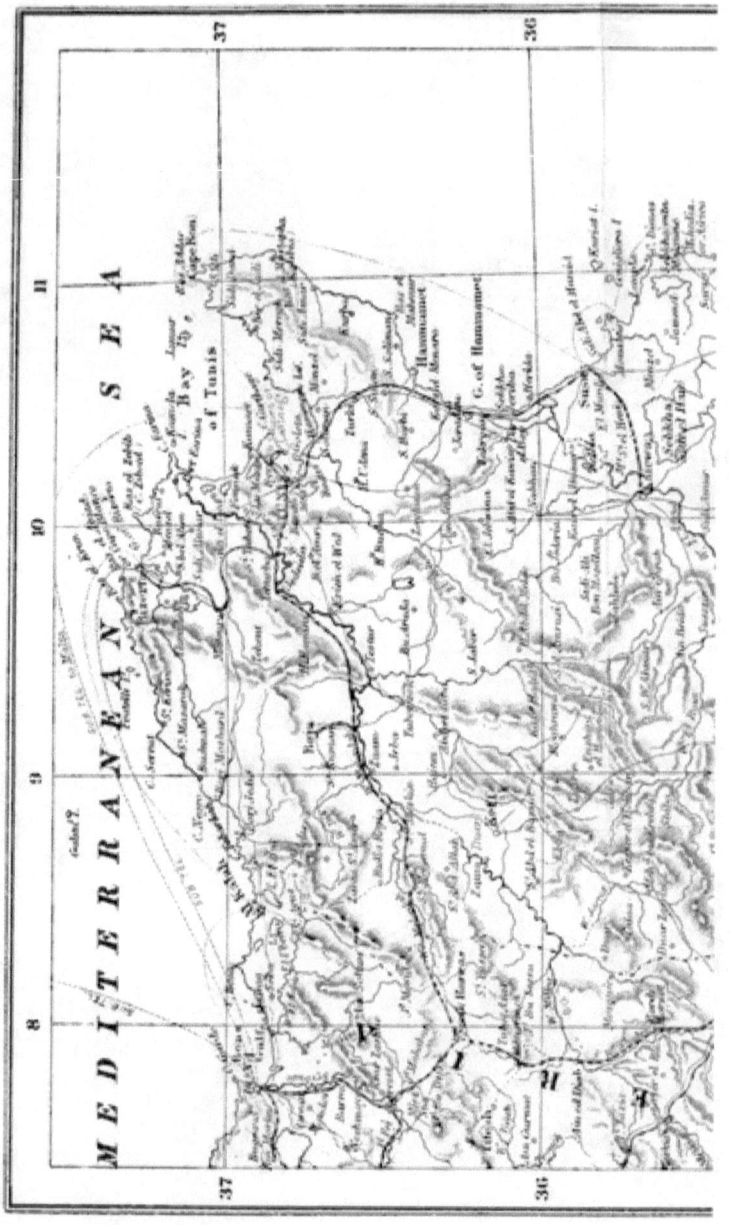

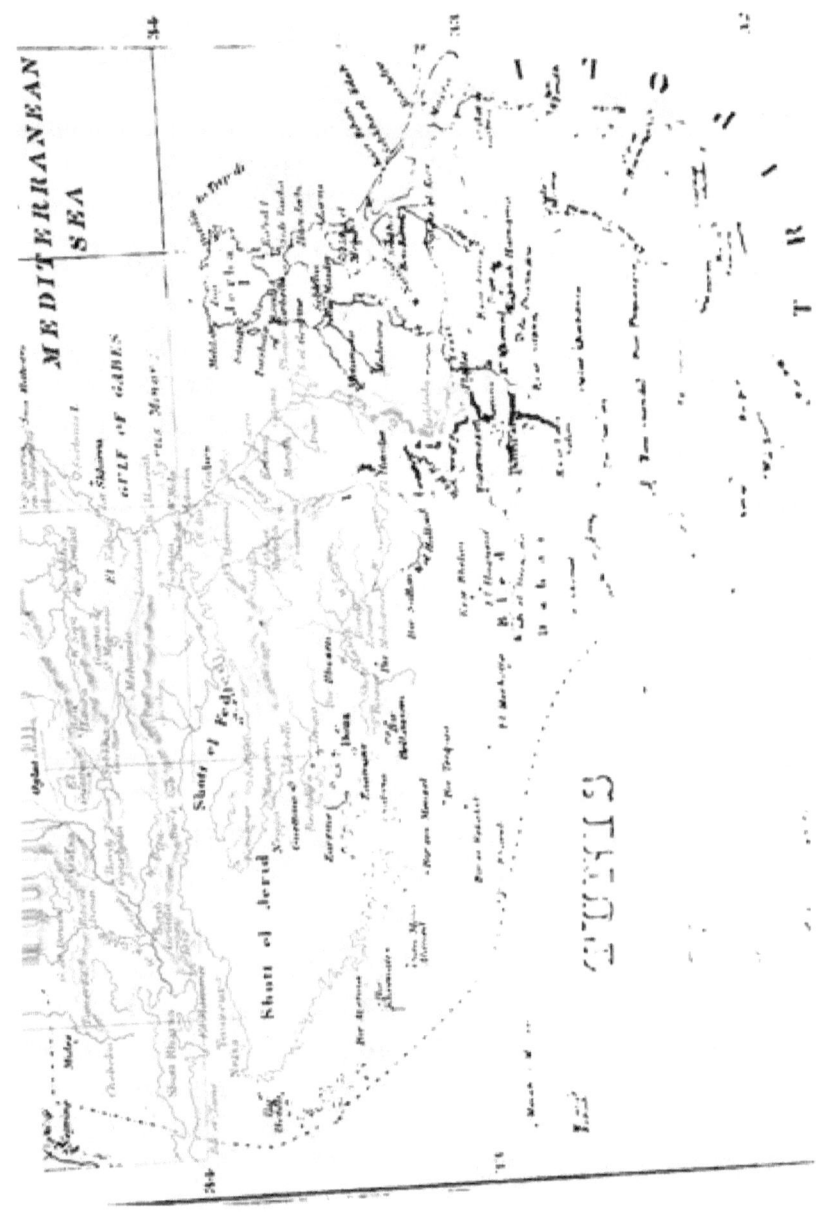

Historical Introduction

The Berbers of Lybia—The Carthaginians (B.C. 1400-146)—A Roman Province (B.C. 146-A.D. 439)—The Vandals (A.D. 439-533)—The Byzantines (A.D. 533-698)—The Arabs (A.D. 698-1573)—The Beys (A.D. 1573-1881).

The Berbers of Lybia. VERY little is known about the original inhabitants of Tunisia. They are all summed up, with the hasty generalization of the ancients, as Berbers or barbarians, and, while some archæologists assure us that they came from the East, others are equally positive that they were an incursion from the West. All that is known about them is that they were strong enough, some thirty-four centuries ago, to attack Egypt, and that on the arrival of the first Phœnician colonists (about 1400 B.C.) they possessed prosperous towns.

The Carthaginians (B.C. 1400-146.) The first Phœnician settlements were few and far between. Like the Portuguese colonies in India during the 16th century, each settlement occupied a port and fortified it towards the land. There was no idea of conquest, and the intention was merely to establish trading centres for the purchase of ivory, gold dust, and ostrich feathers, which remain the principal exports of Africa to the present day. Even

Carthage was founded (about 800 B.C.) by Queen Dido merely for purposes of commerce. It was not till the 6th century B.C. that a Carthaginian kingdom could be said to exist. It proved this existence by the rapidity of its colonial expansion, and it was soon master of the Mediterranean. Excepting for a repulse in Sicily, everything smiled upon its arms until it came into collision with Rome, with whom it was engaged in a death struggle, lasting from 264 to 146 B.C. The first Carthaginian war ended in 241 B.C. with the expulsion of the Carthaginians from Sicily and the payment of a heavy tribute. In the next war Hannibal penetrated to the very gates of Rome; but the Romans, disregarding the imminence of their danger, despatched Scipio to attack Carthage, and his successes necessitated the recall of Hannibal just when he seemed on the eve of final victory. The two generals met at Zama on the 19th October, 202 B.C., when Scipio gained one of the few decisive battles in the history of the world.

It is one sign of the hopelessness of the attempt to recognise any trace of ancient history in modern Tunisia that the very site of this great battle is still in dispute. Every sort of historical and archæological discovery might be revealed by proper enterprise, or even by taking a spade and digging it almost anywhere at random a few feet below the surface. But so long as the French remain there, and are permitted to retain their dog-in-the-manger attitude, we shall never learn anything.

The battle of Zama reduced Carthage to the position of a vassal of Rome, and when in 149 B.C. Massinissa, King of Numidia, invaded Carthaginian territory, a motion of resistance was pronounced to be an infringement of the suzerainty. Rome protested, and Carthage abased herself once more, yielding up hostages and a large proportion of her arms. But when Rome went on to decree the destruction of Carthage, she awoke to the courage of despair, and a last desperate struggle was determined upon. The bronze of the temples, the woodwork of the palaces, and the ornaments of the people were devoted to the construction of fresh arms; the women cut off their hair and contributed it for bow-strings and catapults; slaves were emancipated, and furnished with weapons to resist the hated tyrant.

At first there seemed to be hope, but another Scipio arrived in the spring of 146 B.C. and beat down the city wall. The struggle still went on in the streets and the houses, until the last brave remnant, setting fire to the Acropolis, perished in the flames, and even the hard conqueror was moved to tears.

Thus the last bulwark against Roman aggression perished, and the city of Dido was razed to the ground. Wandering among her ruins to-day, and observing a foot or two beneath the soil the telltale layer of cinders, it is impossible not to realize the completeness of the Roman vandalism, or to withhold a tribute of indignation to the completeness of this barbarous conquest.

It was long before the Roman conquest was complete. A solitude was created and given the name of peace. When at last anything in the nature of reconstructive energy was permitted, the Romans, like the Latin race, which has now succeeded them in possession of the country, concerned themselves only with their own enrichment and the enslavement of the natives. An army of occupation, amounting to fully 30,000 men, and an army of officials on a monstrously extravagant scale covered the country like locusts. Roads, aqueducts, monuments, theatres, were called into being by the forced labour of the conquered race for the sole enjoyment of their task-masters. As the central authority of Rome grew weaker, insurrection after insurrection occurred to trouble her African Empire. Again and again the independence of the region was proclaimed for varying periods. At last, in 417 A.D., a final revolt of the Berbers, now a more mixed race than ever, paved the way for the incursion of Genseric and his Vandals.

<small>A Roman Province. (B.C. 146 A.D. 439.)</small>

Seizing Carthage, which the Romans had rebuilt, Genseric used it, with a kind of poetic justice, as a base from which he proceeded to avenge the long tale of wrongs, which they had inflicted upon the country. He employed the natives to participate in his ravaging onslaughts on Europe; but his work in the world was solely one of destruction, and his people never took any root in the soil or possessed it outside their encamp-

<small>The Vandals. A.D. 439-533.)</small>

ROMAN AQUEDUCT NEAR THE BARIM.

ments. Tunisia could only be controlled by the iron hand of a great warrior, and the successors of Genseric found themselves unable to cope with the revolts of Berbers who had learnt the art of war at their hands. Profiting by these constantly recurring troubles, and by a dispute over the Vandal succession, the Emperor Justinian despatched an armament under Belisarius, who entered Carthage in triumph after a campaign of eight days (September, 533).

The characteristic of the Byzantine domination was revealed by this rapidity of conquest. A firm government was immediately set up, and the fortresses which had been dismantled were restored to more than their original strength. But the utmost resources of the Empire and the repeated campaigns of her most famous generals could not avail to pacify the Berbers, who were scarcely subdued in one place when they broke out in another. They had come very near obtaining their independence when, in 647, an Arab invasion brought about one more change in the mastery of the country. The people welcomed this, in the same way that they had welcomed the Vandal invasion, as a respite from oppression, and did all they could to facilitate its triumph. The Arabs were at first bought off, but they constantly re-appeared, and soon showed signs of consolidating their conquests. In 670 they built the foundations of their future capital at Kairwàn, and in 698 were masters of the whole country.

The Byzantines. (A.D. 533-698.)

But for the presence of the French, the Tunisia

of to-day cannot differ very widely from that of the Arab domination in the 11th century. It is to that noblest and most picturesque portion of the human race that we owe the changelessness of the golden East. The Arabs brought with them the most perfect traditions of chivalry, the sublimest architecture, the most delicate art, and the most glorious simplicity which the world may ever know. After the gross tyranny of Rome, the coarseness of the Vandals, and the corruption of the Byzantines, lo, a dainty sunrise succeeding to the horrors of a murky night! A millennium of romance had replaced the petty struggles of a series of commercial conquerors. The Berbers were not likely to remain quiet for long under any foreign domination, and we find many dramatic incidents in a protracted rebellion led by a martial Jewess, named El-kahina (the Cohen, or priestess), a great general, and a surprising stateswoman, at a period and in a country where women were classed among the beasts that perish. But nothing and nobody could long withstand the triumph of the Arab administration, whose glories, both in peace and war, constituted the golden age of Tunisia. The empire of the Arabs stretched to the confines of Egypt and to the uttermost parts of Morocco. Charles the Great sent a friendly embassage to request the surrender of the relics of African martyrs, and his wishes were met in a spirit of the most charming courtesy. For over 500 years (972–1535) the country was permitted to enjoy the benefits of native Moslem dynasties, under the vassalage of the Arabs. Then

The Arabs.
(A.D. 698-1573.)

for a short period the country acknowledged the suzerainty of Charles V., until, in 1573, a Turkish kingdom of Tunis was constituted under the administration of a Dey.

The Beys.
(A.D. 1573-1381.)
In Tunisia, as in most other portions of the Turkish Empire, the unruliness of the janissaries turned the Turkish government into a tyranny. A Bey or Dey was elected for life, and depended upon a divan of three hundred members. This was the golden age of the Barbary corsairs, whose traditions have continued down to the memory of living men. The strange thing about this period is perhaps the complaisance of Europe, tolerating a nest of pirates, which never possessed more than fourteen war-ships and yet contrived to terrorise the whole Mediterranean. The government of the Beys was a period of internal as well as of external turmoil until 1705, when the elective Beys came to an end, and Hussein succeeded in founding a dynasty, which continues to occupy the throne nominally at the present day. Never, even at the period of its foundation, was the government of the Beys an effective one. It contented itself with a kind of military promenade twice a year, administering a sort of justice on its passage, but concerning itself more particularly with the collection of exorbitant taxes. It was not until after the defeat of Buonaparte at Waterloo, that Europe had leisure to concern herself with the minor misdemeanours of the Barbary pirates, and even then she contented herself with friendly treaties for the release of Chris-

tian slaves. Only after the accession of the Bey Ahmed, in 1837, his foolish attempts to Europeanize himself and his country, and the financial embarrassment which naturally ensued, did the fall of the Beylicate loom in sight. Then, under the weak government of his successors, the usual pretexts of security and reform were seized, and, Lord Salisbury having made a weak concession to the French at the Congress of Berlin, France took an early opportunity of virtually annexing the country.

In 1881 an unimportant rising of the Krumir tribe was seized upon as a pretext for invasion. French troops, acting nominally in the interests of the Bey, advanced upon the rebels, who gave way at once, whereupon the real object of the expedition was avowed and the Bey was given two hours to sign a treaty, handing over the foreign policy and internal administration of his country to the French, who proceeded to put down all resistance with a heavy hand.

Chapter I
THE BEY

The Prisoner of Marsa—A French Puppet—A State Prisoner—The Puppet's Shadow of State—Appearance—The Heir—A Modern Sovereign—The Palace at Marsa—The Bodyguard—The Gardens—The Menagery—The Palace at Tunis—The Bardo

The Prisoner at Marsa. A VISIT to His Highness Ali, Bey of Tunis, is like a visit to an extinct volcano. A constitutional monarch reigns, but does not govern: it is as much as ever if the Bey may be said to reign. Decrees still issue in his name, but he is scarcely apprised of them beforehand, certainly not consulted. The French Government, which is to him what a democratic parliament is to a constitutional monarch, and more also, uses his name as a bugbear for discontented Moslems or jealous foreign powers, but takes care to efface his personality as much as possible. You may spend weeks in the Regency and remain unconvinced of his existence in this French dependency. Should you chance to be near the Italian railway station of Tunis on a Monday morning, you may witness the arrival of a portly old gentleman, who hurries into a ramshackle mediæval carriage with a bellagged escutcheon on the door, and drives off to Dar-el-Bey as fast as his pair of white mules can carry him.

A French Puppet. Here he receives any French officials who may have instructions for him; but he dislikes the humiliation of this procedure, and makes his stay as short as possible, anxious to return at the earliest moment to the monotony of his palace at Marsa. It is significant of his relations with the French authorities that they make him come to them in this way, and will under no circumstances pay him the compliment of a visit to his house, even when the Resident is at his summer quarters hard by. Foreign representatives are no longer accredited to him, but to the French Republic; and they may spend years at Tunis without seeing more of him than does the Cook's tourist, whose guide takes him to the station to watch the passage of His Highness. The relations between him and the French are the merest farce. He speaks nothing but Arabic, and his interpreter, General Valensi, a Levantine Hebrew, who has been admitted to French citizenship, knows Arabic and French with equal imperfection. Monday's ceremony consists of little more than the interchange of perfunctory inquiries about the state of their health between the Bey and the Resident, or his representative; various documents are produced for His Highness's signature, which is given without any attempt to master their contents, and the trying ceremony is at an end.

A State Prisoner. The French take good care to discourage all applications for audiences of the Bey, and, except on the rare occasion of his weekly visit to the Dar-el-Bey, His Highness rarely sees any one, except the members of his own family. Indeed, he is to all intents and purposes a State prisoner, solaced by a civil list of £37,500 a year. Your request for an audience is met by the reply that the Bey is now a very old man, and that it would be too much to ask him to receive visitors. Until recently, however, his wife—he has but one—was permitted to receive the wives of distinguished strangers in the harem at Marsa, but this she has now had to discontinue. She is a Circassian, and is said to have been very beautiful once upon a time. The late Bey had sent to the East to buy her for his harem, but died while she was on her way. The present Bey took a fancy to her when she arrived, and married her. It is almost an Arabic version of the Duke of York's romance.

The Puppet's Shadow of State. The only occasion when you may hope to come in contact with the Bey of Tunis is during the days of Bairam, the Moslem holiday which follows the fast of Ramadan. Then he repairs to the palace of the Bardo, two or three miles out of Tunis, and receives all comers. The French Resident and the General in command of the French forces don their cocked hats and their orders, and drive in state, with outriders and a guard of cavalry, to wish him the compliments of the season. There is always a great concourse of people, with jugglers, snake-charmers, strolling minstrels, itinerant vendors of nuts and sherbet, and all the other concomitants of Moslem revelry. You elbow your way into the large hall of justice, where the Bey is seated on a gilt throne upholstered with red velvet. It is here that, on rare occasions, he is still privileged to come and give his assent to the execution of an Arab criminal in the field hard by. You are struck by the want of ceremony observed. The crowds of French officials are all chatting together, and make no effort to avoid turning their backs to the straw sovereign. Their chief pre-occupation seems to be to avoid contact with the native dignitaries, who slouch about in ill-fitting European costumes and the *sheshia*—a low fez with a long blue tassel, their only remnant of Oriental dress.

Appearance. The Bey himself wears plain trousers and a richly-embroidered frock-coat with epaulettes, not unlike a naval officer's uniform. Across his breast is the ribbon of the Order of the Blood, the Tunisian Garter, which is confined to some seventeen persons, mostly of royal rank. He wears also a constellation of foreign orders, a sword whose hilt is encrusted with jewels, and a *sheshia*, covered with gold embroidered leaves and precious stones. His predecessor was the first Bey to adopt this semblance of European costume, and strict Moslems ascribe his humiliation largely to it. His face is ruddy, and he wears a closely-trimmed white beard, whiskers and moustache; his expression is benevolent, but weak and by no means intelligent. He seems scarcely to take in the compliments of the French Resident, clumsily translated to him by General Valensi.

"*Hamdou lillah* (God be praised), I am well. What is the health of your Excellency?" is his constant refrain, repeated with all the variations in vogue at

Tunis. The Resident remarks that His Highness wore a fur coat to come to the Bardo, and trusts that His Highness did not feel the cold. "No, *hamdou lillah*, I did not feel the cold. It was my son who compelled me to wrap myself up." And a faint smile plays upon the expressionless lips. Poor Bey! His attention often wanders, and you realize that he is thinking of the contempt he must excite among his compatriots.

The Heir. Taib Bey,[1] his brother and heir-apparent, is close by, and watches him with a flash of pity in his deep-set eyes. You have heard that he is disaffected towards the French, and you wonder how he would have comported himself in Ali's place—how he will comport himself when his time shall come. Alas, it is too late!

A Modern Sovereign. It is on the second and third days of Bairam that the Bey shows to best advantage, when he is receiving the homage of his subjects,—subjects who might have been. There are traces of the old patriarchal demeanour, and you reflect upon a sovereign who might have been a father and a friend to his people. Sometimes his eyes, dulled with age and disappointment, light up as he converses with one of the heroes of the war against the French or a noted intriguer, but they always encounter some emissary of the Residency, and quickly resume their shifty stare, which would be pathetic if it were not contemptible.

The Palace at Marsa. By dint of pertinacity you may obtain permission to visit the palace of Marsa.

[1] Since deceased.

The French would far rather you refrained from thus gratifying your curiosity; but if you insist, they deem it wiser to place no obstacle. General Valensi writes you out a permit in scratchy Arabic, and you present it to a slouching sentinel, who leaves you in the doorway for many minutes while he goes to verify the document. The French attaché, who has taken care to accompany you, sneers at the delay, and remarks that the Bey's household think it adds to their importance if they keep Europeans waiting.

<small>The Bodyguard.</small> The delay gives you an opportunity of observing the Bey's bodyguard at exercise in the wide courtyard. They drill badly, and even their goose-step is execrable. A file of Brighton school girls were more military in keeping step; but the men are well-built and evidently good fighting material. They go through various evolutions around shiny cannons, which the French attaché ridicules as toys. Meanwhile, you are struck by the slipshod aspect of the place, the sentinels gossiping and smoking at their posts, the unkempt uniforms, the procession of scullions, with dirty dishes and barrowsful of refuse, through the principal entrance of the palace.

<small>The Gardens.</small> At last your emissary returns, and you are conducted through the gardens. There are large enclosures full of cabbages and burrage, lemon groves, tawdry summer-houses and hideous rockeries, arrays of untidy cottage flowers, and gravelled walks bordered with orange tulips and overgrown with weeds. On a flat roof against the skyline is a gaunt

SQUARE OUTSIDE THE DAR-EL-BEY.

camel trudging painfully round a small circle to draw up water from a well.

The Menagery. The menagery is the most interesting feature of the place, and the one in which the Bey chiefly delights. A black bear and a hyena are confined each in a cruelly narrow cage, and you are not surprised at their bad temper. The hyena managed to escape at feeding time not long ago, and spread consternation throughout the gardens, particularly among the gazelles, which are special favourites of the Bey. They are kept in a large yard, thickly covered with sand, which is intended to remind them of their native deserts. They seem in excellent condition, but do not display the tameness you have observed among gazelles accustomed to be treated as pets. One of them is particularly shy and grows very restive when a young Arab seizes it by the horns to enforce a caress. He explains that it is moping for the loss of a sister, whose corpse you presently perceive outstretched upon the gravel walk. Surely there is no sight more pathetic than that of a dead gazelle. You remark that its eyes have been removed, and you learn that they were demanded by one of the attendants of the Bey's wife, as there is a superstition that those who eat them acquire beautiful eyes. In the same enclosure as the gazelles are a number of Sahara sheep, strangest and clumsiest of animals, standing in corners and staring with frightened gaze. The Arabs say they are possessed by the souls of the wicked, and their appearance certainly bears out that theory. You make the acquaintance of a comical baboon, which caresses his keeper with a great show of affection; you sniff at the cage of a civet cat, which exhales an agreeable odour of musk to a distance of several yards; and you enter the aviary, which is remarkably well stocked. A couple of large pelicans look delightfully wise and ridiculous with their prodigious bills, and some pheasant peacocks are pointed out as rarities, in striking contrast to the homely guinea pigs in hutches hard by.

The Palace at Tunis. The Dar-el-Bey (House of the Bey) at Tunis and the Bardo palace outside are now little more than show-places, bearing the stamp of disuse firmly imprinted on every room. The charm of each lies in the patios and the arabesques. The patios, as in every Arab house, are wide, pillared courtyards of black and white marble, either open to the sky or roofed with glass. They are in the centre of a house, and all the rooms are approached through them. When there is a fountain at play in the centre, they convey a delicious sense of coolness and luxury. The arabesques are carved in white plaster, and the fancifulness of their designs is particularly artistic. Sometimes they take the place of windows, and a background of coloured glass confers the most fantastic effects. Alas! the art of making arabesques is fast dying out, for the French despise them and the Arabs have almost ceased building. As it takes a man all day to work a piece of arabesque the size of your hand, they are obviously expensive. You are told that only two makers of arabesques still survive, that they are very old, and that when they die they will have no successors.

PANORAMA FROM THE DAR-EL-BEY.

While visiting the Dar-el-Bey you must not omit to climb up to the flat roof, which commands one of the finest panoramas of the white city glistening in the sunshine, and where you are at close quarters with the muezzins of neighbouring minarets. The rooms themselves are bare, save for an occasional gilt throne or ragged divan shrouded in chintz covers. In one of the principal halls you may, however, admire at every window an ingenious peep-hole, through which former Beys were enabled to perceive the concourse in the bazaar without themselves being perceived. And the ceilings are a constant delight. That in the dining-hall is covered with arabesques of very graceful patterns, while others are of carved wood, vividly but exquisitely painted in green and gold and red.

The Bardo. The palace of the Bardo is even more dilapidated and desolate than the Dar-el-Bey. The great courtyard is full of refuse, and the harem has been turned into a museum of no particular interest. The walls of the saloons are mostly covered with badly executed portraits of Victor Emmanuel, Louis Napoleon Buonaparte and recent Beys. You are perhaps chiefly struck by the unnecessary profusion of ormolu clocks. In one room I counted no less than fifteen, all of gigantic proportions, and not one of them going. Were they all wound up, the chorus of their ticks would assuredly be distracting.

The Bey's life at Marsa, if it is uneventful, is not unhappy. He rises late and retires early, and the short days soon pass away, divided as they are between prayers in his private mosque, lengthy meals, drives in the neighbourhood, and strolls among his animals. No one has anything but praise for his kindness of heart and invariable geniality. He showed in 1881 that he could take an active part if need be, for he commanded a column against his own subjects when they resisted the French. But at his advanced age there is no need to wonder if he prefers the repose and security which the shortcomings of his predecessors have imposed.

BARDO PALACE: IRON STAIRCASE.

Chapter II

THE MODERN BARBARY PIRATES

French Administration—Finance—Taxes—Army—Unlike Algeria—Tunisia has an Astute Despotism—The Official Version—Is highly coloured—Exactions of Officials—A Great Gulf Fixed—Travel Hindered — Spy-Mania — Communications — Camp Followers, not Colonists — Vexatious Custom-Houses — The Future of the Country—Our Lost Opportunity.

French Administration. THE Bey retains a Prime Minister and a Minister of the Pen, who are practically under the orders of M. Millet, the French Resident, who is nominally subject to the Foreign Minister of the Republic, but has hitherto enjoyed a fairly free hand. He is a self-made man and somewhat of a rough diamond. His assistant, M. Révoil, is more of the gentleman and the diplomatist, but generally resides in France while M. Millet is at Tunis, merely replacing him during his absence. There is a staff of attachés at the Residency, but they seem to do little more than clerical work, unless specially delegated to any mission by the Resident. The work of administration throughout the country is done by a number of French prefects, known as contrôleurs civils, who supervise and bully the kaids, or native administrators, as the Resident does the Bey. ' Big fleas have little fleas. .' The kaids occupy themselves with the native police, the collection of taxes, and certain military and judicial functions, assisted by minor officials known as khalifas and sheikhs. The contrôleur has all the authority and the kaïd most of the responsibility. In the tribal districts the old patriarchal administration remains, subject, of course, to the ceaseless interference of the contrôleur. Several towns have also a municipal administration, the Arabs being under an official who is generally the local kaïd, and the Jews being under one of their own race.

Finance. The real cause of the fall of the Tunisian monarchy was, as usual, a reckless system of finance. In 1870 the interest on the debt amounted to nineteen and a half million francs, while the total revenue of the Regency amounted only to thirteen and a half millions. Then a French, English and Italian Commission effected a composition with the creditors; but even after reducing the debt by one half, the Regency was still unable to pay interest regularly until the time of the Protectorate. The French Government, by guaranteeing future Tunisian emissions, effected a series of conversions, and has by now restored the position of the finances. The old Commission, in which Italy and England had a share, was not unnaturally terminated, and the French took over the entire administration of the finances. The principal items of the present expenditure are £255,600 for interest on the debt, £190,480 for public works, £67,200 for the civil list of the Bey and his family, £38,560 for the post office, £30,480 for education, £27,200 for contrôleurs civils and agriculture, besides heavy extraordinary expenses which amounted to £177,080 in 1894. The French claim to have spent a large sum of their own money, amounting to no less than eleven and a half millions sterling, up to 1896, but this includes the expenses of military expeditions against Tunisia and all the expenses of the army of occupation, which would in any case have had to be maintained elsewhere. By a reasonable calculation, the French expenses connected with Tunisia cannot be set down at more than £32,000 a year, and efforts are constantly being made to transfer every possible portion of it from the French to the Tunisian taxpayer.

Taxes. Under the Beys, taxation was irregularly collected; for several years a man might pay nothing at all; then of a sudden he might be mulcted of most of his savings. Now he knows exactly what he will have to pay, but it often amounts to more than ever; and when he reflects that the natives have to bear the whole burden of the occupation (military expenses alone excepted), it is not surprising that he should murmur. It is true that he has obtained facilities for exporting his corn to France, but the money value of this is difficult to bring home to him, particularly at a time when four bad seasons in succession have reduced his crops till they barely suffice for his own needs. The chief source of revenue is the *mejba*, a poll tax of 16s. a year on every adult male, which swallows sometimes as much as a quarter of the whole income of a working man. A native also owes three days of forced labour to the government, and there are heavy taxes upon the production of all cereals and oils, as well as taxes on every olive and palm tree in the Regency. Gardens, rents, freeholds, are also heavily taxed—one sixteenth of every rent being due to the government—while industry and commerce are subjected not merely to export and import dues, but to an infinite variety of complicated taxes known as *ma'sulats*.

Army. At the time of the occupation the Bey had an army organized on the French pattern, but so costly that the pay was always hopelessly in arrear. In 1883 it was reduced to a bodyguard of 600 men, including a band, and the total cost per annum is only £24,600. There is now a conscription for young men between eighteen and twenty-two, and the service is for two years. The two Tunisian regiments thus recruited are numbered as if they formed part of the Algerian army. There are also three French regiments and two French battalions, which, with the two native regiments, make up a total of 14,473 men under the command of the Minister of War.

A French officer, who has seen service in Tunisia, gave me details of the discipline in the south. The favourite punishment is known as *crapaudine*. It consists of spreading out a soldier, like a toad, against the wall of a punishment cell, with his outstretched arms and legs securely tied, and leaving him there for two or three days without food or water. As the weather is generally very hot in those regions, the tortures of thirst are terrible, and the punishment is much dreaded. Not long ago a soldier died under the treatment, and there was some scandal; but the officers pleaded that strong measures were absolutely necessary for maintaining discipline, and that the only alternative would be frequent executions. Another favourite punishment is to strip a man, tie his legs, and expose him all day to the sun in the desert. In extreme cases also men have been tied to a horse's tail, and dragged at a gallop through the sand. The strange thing is, that the men do not make loud protest when their comrades are punished in these ways; but if there were any attempt to introduce flogging, it would certainly be followed by a mutiny, as corporal punishment would be considered an intolerable indignity. When I mentioned that flogging was not unknown in our service, my informant could not conceal his amazement. Appointments in the outposts of Tunisia are in great demand among the officers, and are considered a sure avenue to advancement. It is a frequent source of complaint with the army of occupation that a mule receives far more consideration from the authorities than a French soldier. A mule costs money to buy while a soldier can be impressed at will; and if ever it becomes a question which of the two shall be spared, it is the mule which has the preference. If the French were logical, no doubt they would follow the Americans in according burial with military honours to all their mules who fell in the field.

<small>Unlike Algeria.</small> In Algeria you find one of the strangest forms of "popular" government in the world.

The French colonists and the native Jews alone have votes, and as there are 47,000 Jews to 270,000 French, the elections are generally swamped by the Jews, who sell their votes to the highest bidder. The suffrage was conferred on them at the instance of a French Jew, named Crémieux, whose proposal was slipped into the Constitution of 1870, when the French assembly had other things to think of, and could not concern itself with intricate racial questions in Algeria.

In Tunisia the government is a despotism, and the French authorities never tire of pointing out that they are there not by conquest but by Treaty. There is a kind of parliament, to be sure, but, like the old pre-Revolutionary parliaments, it possesses only consultative powers. It may pass what resolutions it pleases, but the Resident may, and often does, merely take note of them. His administration, with infinite astuteness, neglects no effort to smooth native susceptibilities. All decrees issue in the name of Allah and his Highness the Bey, and are merely countersigned by M. Millet, their originator. When it is necessary to modify some ancient national institution, the thing is done with the utmost delicacy. For instance, difficulties had been caused by a species of mortmain. Religious corporations, known as *habbus*, hold land inalienably, and a law of the Medes and Persians absolutely forbids the sale of it in any circumstances. The French Government has accordingly announced its intention to respect this law in theory, but it enacts that henceforward *habbu* land

Tunisia has an astute Despotism.

may be "exchanged for money." A long stay in Tunis is not needed to realize how cleverly the French throw dust in the eyes of the Tunisians: taking the Bey's name in vain to overawe his subjects, modifying fundamental laws by quibbles, and exercising a stern despotism under the guise of a disinterested Protectorate. But it requires some weeks' steady exploration of the interior to perceive that the Government is no less adroit in blinding the ingenuous traveller. While I remained in the capital I heard the authorised version so often, and from such varied and unimpeachable sources, that it seemed almost impossible to doubt.

<small>The Official Version</small> All asserted in chorus that, whereas twenty years ago it was dangerous to venture outside the gates of the principal towns unarmed, a child might now wander anywhere from the Mogods to the Troglodytes in perfect security with a purse of gold in its hand; that the traveller's only cause for alarm lay in the suspicious nature of the Kabyle dogs, whose bark was, however, worse than their bite; that the one desire of the authorities was to open up the whole Regency as a tourists' playground; that the people were prosperous and contented, as they had never been since the days of the Romans; and that the material blessings of civilization were being propagated hand in hand with the noblest principles of liberty and fraternity.

<small>Is highly Coloured.</small> It is not, of course, to be denied that Tunisia has progressed in many ways under the French; but the picture is, to say the least,

highly coloured. A British Vice-Consul, who has lived many years in remoter Tunisia, told me that, if anything, he had found the country safer before the occupation had aroused race hatreds. In old days he rarely carried a weapon; now he would feel unsafe inland without one, particularly if he carried money with him. From another source I learn that robberies are now frequent in the neighbourhood of Gabes, merchants (especially Jews) being relieved of their purses by masked men, but not otherwise molested. A few weeks before my visit some Arabs had been stopped, and their three camels carried off. This state of things is generally ascribed to hard times, as the Tunisians rarely rob except under the impulse of want.

Exactions of Officials. I have not stayed long enough in Tunisia to know the full iniquity of the French treatment of the natives, but I know that gross cases of extortion are not unusual. A few years ago a French minister came to visit Kairwân in state, and was amazed to find the greater part of the French colony collected on the roofs to greet him with hisses and hoots, and a local variety of "rough music." He was as much surprised as he was put out by his reception, which he had done nothing to earn; and it was not until some time afterwards that he discovered that this was intended as a demonstration against the French Government of Tunisia. The fact was that the colonists were annoyed at the recent removal of a contrôleur, who had facilitated their exactions. They had grabbed the land of the

natives, seized any flocks which happened to stray
there, and exacted monstrous ransoms before they
would give them up; the contrôleur had given
decisions in their favour, in consideration of going
shares with them, and they were accordingly furious
at his removal. In this case the scandal had been
so great that the Government had felt compelled
to intervene; but there are plenty of cases of similar
terrorism, which have not yet reached a sufficient
pitch of notoriety to induce the authorities to put
them down.

A Great Gulf Fixed. The French often express surprise that the Arabs do not accept the privilege of being naturalized as French subjects, which is freely open to them; but at present they cannot do so without virtually abandoning their race and creed. If the French were willing to let them keep their marriage laws and various domestic customs, many of them would, no doubt, be willing to serve in the French army, and pay their share of the taxation. But this the French colonists, who are very jealous about retaining the whole administration of government in their own hands, have not shown any anxiety to facilitate. The Jews, on the other hand, would do anything to avoid the liability of having to fight, but some of them would welcome the extension of the Algerian system to Tunisia.

Travel hindered. Travellers, who attempt to explore Tunisia, will find that the authorities are far more friendly to them in words than in deeds. British ladies, engaged in missionary work in Tunisia, have told me that they have experienced constant annoyance and discourtesy at the hands of the French officials. One of them was summoned for the heinous offence of lending a Bible to a native, and after spending many hours in court, and hearing various persons sentenced to imprisonments for assaults and robberies, was fined 15 francs and costs.[1] It appears that the sale and even loan of books are regulated by straining the Press laws, which are very strict. Whatever we may think of the wisdom of discouraging missions to people who believe fervently in a creed admirably suited to their needs, we surely cannot hear without protest of the persecution of our fellow countrywomen, however indiscreet, for the harmless pastime of lending devotional works.

Spy-mania.
There is, moreover, ample evidence that the spy-mania has spread from France to the Protectorate. All foreigners are subjected to constant espionage by the police, and elaborate *dossiers*, detailing their minutest actions and movements, are stored at the Residency. Sportsmen in pursuit of mouflons near the military outposts are viewed with special suspicion; and all travellers who penetrate out of the beaten track are liable to an annoying supervision, such as would be resented in Russia or Turkey. Even in the streets of Sfax, Mrs. Vivian and I were stopped by the police, who told us that they would assuredly have conducted us to the brigade if I had not chanced to have my passport with me. A similar

[1] She and a friend have since suffered six days' imprisonment (in 1899) for a repetition of the "crime."

incident happened to Sir Lambert Playfair, when he was British Consul-General in Tunis. He had no passport with him, and it was merely by offering to write himself out one that he escaped arrest. Having a large experience of French methods, he was wont to take up a coin and read out the legend thus: "*Liberté point. Egalité point. Fraternité point.*" As to French liberty in Tunisia, it is instructive to note that the Resident stopped all telegrams sent by the correspondents of French journals with reference to the anti-Semitic disturbances at Tunis in 1898.

Communications. It is strange that after directing the destinies of Tunisia so long, the French should have done so little to improve the communications. Railways are few and rickety, diligences are a ruinous torture; and, though the main roads are fairly good, driving upon them in worn-out cabs is by no means a pleasure. For the journey along the coast, the Italian service of boats is by no means uncomfortable, chiefly, perhaps, because it is so poorly patronized; but any attempt to penetrate beyond the mere fringe of the coast, can only be made after purchasing tents, horses, mules, large stores of provisions, and hiring a retinue of guards and attendants, such as are required for exploring the wilds. As for the security of such an undertaking, there is, probably, little danger to be feared from the Arabs, except in the remoter regions; but the traveller will find constant discouragement from the French authorities, whose courtesy leaves much to be desired.

I travelled from Kairwân to Susa by a tramway, and found it extremely uncomfortable. It consists of an open car with abrupt benches for some twelve, or, at a pinch, fourteen passengers. It runs with much rumbling and swaying on rails of 18-in. or 20-in. gauge, drawn by a pair of horses, cantering on a rough track by the side. Whenever we crossed a *wed*, or torrent bed, the rails went over it, unsupported, through the air, while the horses struggled through deep mud or over boulders, sometimes as much as 10 ft. below. I should think accidents would be very easy; but no doubt the tramway will be little used, now that it has to bear the competition of a railway line. A bitterly cold wind completed the miseries of the journey through forty miles of bleak moor, relieved only by occasional patches of bright flowers.

I had intended to go from Susa to Sfax by diligence, despite the warnings of my friends at Tunis, who had tried it. But I found that it would cost 60 francs to take a coupé, and 6 or 7 francs more for luggage, while a carriage could be hired to cover the whole distance of eighty miles for 70 francs. Moreover, the diligences are great, unwieldy edifices, not unlike Noah's ark in appearance. Their wheels are loose, their seats are hard, and, after watching one of them lurch past El Jem, I rejoiced exceedingly that I had not passed the night at its mercy.

It is useless for the French to profess to desire the opening up of Tunisia by tourists, while they make no effort to render travel possible with comparative comfort and cheapness. As things stand at present, they will not lure many people far beyond the capital.

The Pattern State. That the French are not good colonists is a commonplace, but they would have us believe that they have made a brilliant exception in the case of Tunisia, which they proudly claim as a pattern state. Such praise is, however, merely comparative. Tunisia may compare favourably with Algeria, whose administration is a compound of corruption and mismanagement, surpassing even that of France herself; and the Regency may possess many advantages over the various other settlements and penal establishments which make up the French colonial system. But its popularity as a colony must be gauged by the fact that less than 200 French colonists can be induced to come over every year. There are plenty of Italians, Maltese, Greeks and other Levantines ready to come and take what they can get; but their presence is often a doubtful acquisition, and the reputation of the colony would be better if they could be persuaded to stay at home.

If Tunisia is to have credit as a French colony, it must be colonized by Frenchmen. This the authorities understand, and they constantly endeavour to devise means whereby French agriculturists may be induced to come. But with the best will in the world they do not contrive to present a very attractive picture. I have in my hand a pamphlet which they have issued for distribution among persons contemplating emigration. It begins by setting forth the superior advantages of Tunisia over America and other fields of colonization: the beneficent climate; the absence of fevers, savages, prairie fires; and the presence of the French flag to afford protection and the feeling of home. But it goes on to lay great stress upon the futility of coming over without capital, intelligence, and industry; the possession of which three blessings would, however, enable most men to do well anywhere, without the need of emigration. There are not even free concessions of land, or subsidies of any kind. Necessaries, with the exception perhaps of bread and the worst imaginable meat, are no cheaper than in the average French provincial town, while all luxuries, down to the very smallest, are infinitely dearer.

Camp-followers, not colonists. Practically, the chief form which French colonization has taken so far, has been little more than a species of camp-following. Wherever a French garrison establishes itself, a number of tawdry shops, rough eating-houses, and dismal places of entertainment creep into existence. No doubt the proprietors rapidly enrich themselves by the sale of inferior goods at prices calculated to repay them for the burthen of expatriation; and if this satisfies the aspirations of French expansion, there is no more to be said.

Vexatious Custom-houses. I may mention an incident which illustrates the working of the French Custom-houses. There is a very severe law, prohibiting the importation of all plants on pain of a heavy fine and imprisonment. A trader at Gabes, desirous of growing roses in his garden, ordered some cuttings from abroad, and they were of course captured at the custom-house. The official who effected the confiscation put the cuttings aside, destining them for his own garden; but another official came along in his absence and carried them off. The first official was furious, and there were endless reports on the subject, none of which led to any practical results. The cuttings, however, were planted in the second official's garden, and have provided the only European roses which are to be found in the locality. The custom-house also prohibits the importation of any bulbs which require to be brought with their native earth. There is a certain bulb produced at Tripoli and largely used in Arab perfumery, but as it cannot travel without earth it is not admitted at the Tunisian ports, though, owing to the fact that no custom-houses exist on the land frontier, these bulbs have long found their way to all the druggists' shops in the Regency. When, however, a man attempted to import them wholesale by land, the Government at once intervened, and confiscated all his supply in spite of every protest.

The Turks encourage free trade between Tripoli and Tunis by land, because they have a law establishing it between provinces of their Empire, from which they have never acquiesced in the exclusion of Tunisia; and the French military authorities, who derive no profit from the customs duties, encourage contraband by land, just as they discourage the collection of taxes within their districts, because they find people more easy to govern when there are no grievances about taxation.

The civil administration must look after itself, and, finding that it would not pay to establish a cordon of custom-houses all along the frontier of Tripoli, takes its chance of being able to lay hands upon any large consignment of smuggled goods which may have made its way in.

The Future of the Country. One thing is certain, that the present anomalous form of government in Tunisia cannot possibly be permanent. Either the French people will insist upon some experiment of representation, and Tunisia will be reduced to the pitiable level of Algeria; or the Arabs, in a wave of religious enthusiasm, will drive the French into the sea; or else a French reverse in Europe will lead to the annexation of the Regency by another of the great powers. The French character does not lend itself to expansion. France cannot colonize, because the decent part of her population prefers to remain at home, and her brief attempts at empire have been mere flashes in the pan. Who, then, will be her successor? Italy has long coveted the country, and still floods it with a large proportion of its colonists; but Italy has not been so successful in attempting to govern herself, that she may be allowed to go on exhibiting her failures elsewhere. Turkey has traditional claims, and can show a clean record in Tripoli; but the restoration of any of her lost provinces would meet with much opposition in the present condition of public opinion. England alone, among those who have definite interests in the Mediterranean, can claim to be considered. The large Maltese population in

Tunisia has already provided us with a foothold, and our success in Egypt and India proves us to be the most obvious instrument for the reasonable civilization and competent administration of Muhammadan races. Many have wondered why we did not establish a sphere of influence there long ago, when it would have been easy, and why we remained mute when the French established themselves there. Our silence, however, appears to have been but one more in the long series of blunders which has gone to make up the foreign policy of Lord Salisbury.

Our Lost Opportunity. It is said, and, even with his genius for evasion, he has never ventured to deny, that he assented to the occupation as a sop in return for our doubtful acquisition of Cyprus. This, however, does not explain, or still less atone for his failure to use Tunis as a retort whenever the French have complained of our presence in Egypt; and the climax of his weakness and incapacity has surely been reached in the case of his recent treaty. It was one thing to assent to a friendly occupation for the support of the Bey, which is still the limit of French avowal, but it was another thing to permit the Regency to degenerate into a mere French province, and again another thing to allow that province to be used as a blow at our commerce.

Whatever Lord Salisbury may have promised the French at the time of the treaty of Berlin, he cannot deny that he has now formally recognised their occupation, and more also. He himself said, in defending his action, that, by international law, when one country took over another, all pre-existing treaties lapsed; and that, as the French Government of Tunisia possessed a far better life than that of the Regency, he thought himself wiser in making terms with the French. This is, however, a rotten chain of argument from beginning to end. In the first place, many authorities hold that when one country takes over another, it is also bound to take over all treaties and liabilities. Secondly, apart from this question, the French say that they have not taken over Tunisia; and Lord Salisbury's treaty therefore concedes to them what they have not yet asked for, and what we ought to fight tooth and nail to prevent their obtaining.

It is the fact of the treaty which is the blunder, not so much the details of it, though they are objectionable enough. The question of cotonnades, for instance, though by no means trivial, is not of paramount interest. As one of the Secretaries at the Residency remarked to me with frank cynicism, these questions are easily arranged: French diplomacy concedes a few centimes on the import of cottons, and we give up a certain number of kilometres in the Niger region. Nor must it be forgotten that we have by this treaty practically surrendered an important market to France. True, there remains a show of our retaining most favoured nation treatment, but there is a clause in our treaty, as in all others recently concluded by the French Government of Tunis, to the effect that this phrase shall not be held to include France. And goods from India, which does not enjoy the benefits of most favoured nation, pay seven times as much as our own.

The history of British diplomacy during the last quarter of a century seems to be one long series of wasted opportunities, and the case of Tunis stands out amongst them all with painful prominence. Every one is agreed that Africa must be the scene of our inevitable life-struggle with France, and, if she has not contrived to make of Tunisia a potent weapon against us, the fault is assuredly not ours.

Chapter III

THE CHILDREN OF THE MORNING

Arabs : (1) of Tunis and the Coast—Costume—Houses—(2) of the Interior—Types—Dwellings—Industries—Costume—(3) of the Oases—Costume—Dwellings—Industries—Troglodytes—Home Life—Harems—Vulgarizing by Civilization—Women's Rights—Marriage — Divorce — Funerals — Food — Water-drinking —Drugs—Of learning Arabic—Greetings—Curses—Proverbs.

EVERYTHING about the Arabs serves to emphasize their innate majesty and dignity, which are just as conspicuous when they go about with rags and bare feet as if they had on the most magnificent cloaks of cloth of gold. The nobility of their expression and the majesty of their gait recall the patriarchs of the Bible and those pastoral kings who must have used much the same plain crooked stick for their sceptres, and laid down the law with the same quiet determination. And their dignity is only equalled by their constant courtesy and kindness. Every stranger is made welcome at their modest dwellings in so open-handed a manner that their hospitality has become proverbial. Just as you have only to set eyes upon a Yankee to know him for an impudent vulgarian, so the first sight of an Arab suffices to convince you that he possesses every instinct of a gentleman.

The Arabs of Tunisia are of a somewhat mixed race, what with Berber and Carthaginian ancestors

and the varied origins of their harems; but they may be roughly divided into three groups: (1) those of Tunis and the coast; (2) of the interior; (3) of the oases.

The Arabs of Tunis and the Coast. At Tunis and along the coasts they are remnants of the ancient civilization of the country, which, oddly enough, increases as you proceed from North to South. At Bizerta you find round skulls and little men, recalling the Bretons and Savoyards. In many towns the descendants of slaves who were captured by the Barbary Corsairs are easily recognisable, and many of the family names such as Ingliz (the Englishman), Maltiz (the Maltese) Genwiz (the Genoese), Christou (the Christian), and Franciz (the Frenchman), testify to their origin.

Costume. The men wear a long blouse, slit at the sides to let the arms through. In summer it is of light silk or cotton, in winter of light Austrian cloth or wool—brown or red stripes for choice. Round the *sheshia* is a long silk or cotton turban, twisted up like a gigantic snake. The slippers have high heels and are elaborately varnished, but are too short for the foot, which must require a good deal of practice for a steady walk. The women wear trousers, of cotton or velvet, embroidered with silver or gold, and little cotton or silk blouses, which do not come down to their waists; as they rarely wear anything more than a cotton knitting underneath, their skin remains visible. On grand occasions, instead of blouses, they wear a vest and zouave of brocaded silk or velvet embroidered with gold. They wear as much jewellery as they can afford, including bracelets on their arms and legs. It is the custom to make up a good deal, staining their eyes and eyebrows with kohl, their hands with henna, their lips and cheeks with rouge.

Men of the lower classes of Tunis wear a cloak of dark brown wool, wide knickerbockers, or a kind of striped petticoat, and turbans of various patterns. The length and colour of the blouse vary all along the coast. At Hammamet it is light brown; at Cape Bon it has red and black stripes; at Susa it is of light yellow and very short. A native can always tell you where a man comes from by looking at his clothes. Over the blouse is a little cloak with a hood and sleeves, which generally hang down the back as an ornament. The women of the lower classes wear blouses like those of the men, but wider and without sleeves and tight at the waist. They are sometimes brown, but oftener half red and half violet, while the poorest content themselves with blue or white cotton.

Houses. At Tunis and all along the coast the people are house dwellers, and the main characteristic is a patio, or central courtyard, with all the rooms opening on to it. Most of the rooms are T-shaped, and at the ends of the bar of the T are huge family beds with a great deal of gilt carving. Towards the streets there are scarcely any windows, and these are always protected against inquisitive eyes by elaborately carved wooden gratings. The flat housetops are the general lounge, and, when the women wish to pay visits to each other, they usually walk across the roofs. Noisy dogs are kept there at nighttime to prevent the possibility of intrusion. The inner walls are generally provided with shiny tiles of very beautiful colours, and in rich houses these are supplemented with exquisite arabesques.

The Arabs of the Interior. Even in the interior the traveller is surprised to notice the lightness of the complexions. If he arrives with the ordinary notion that all Orientals are a kind of nigger, it will be a revelation to find that the darkest are scarcely swarthier than the average Spaniard or Italian, and that many would be considered fair in England.

Types. There are two main types: (1) the purer Arab type, found chiefly in the fertile plains of the Mejerda, Siliana, Sers, etc., which are very sparsely populated, and afford one of the many opportunities for colonization which the French have persistently neglected. The chief characteristics are a narrow, beak-like nose, thin lips, a retreating chin, and large, almond-shaped eyes. (2) The Ibero-Numidian type, found in the forests of Krumeria and the Mogod country, as well as in the Southern districts of Tunisia. The foreheads are high and narrow, there is a hollow between the eyes, and the jaws are heavy. Many members of this type are descended from the Moors, who took refuge in Tunisia after their expulsion from Spain, and many of them spoke Spanish down to the end of last century.

Dwellings. They have a high standard of comfort, and live either in picturesque villages or in lofty canvas tents divided up into several rooms. Some of them prefer the *gurbi*, a kind of cabin, which marks the stage of development between a tent and a house. It is not unlike a cattle-shed, composed of wooden posts and thick heaps of brushwood, the floor of the rooms being excavated some two feet below the surface.

GURGU DOORWAY.

Industries. Their industries are exceedingly primitive. The women weave the hair of goats and camels into mats, and the men carve sticks, flutes, spoons, sabots, etc., in geometrical designs. They all make rough pots, which they bake themselves.

TUNISIA

Costume. All Arab countrywomen wear what answers to the ancient Greek *peplos*. It is composed of two separate pieces of blue blanket, one worn in front and the other behind. These are not

GURBI.

sewn together at all, but are pinned to the shoulder by a rude silver brooch. For further security they wear a red girdle, tied at the side to a copper ring. On the head is a turban with a floating veil, which covers the head and shoulders. In their ears are huge silver hoops, tied by strings to their turbans, as the weight would otherwise injure their ears. Round the neck is a collar supporting every sort of ornament and amulet, hands of Fatima in copper or silver, pieces of coral

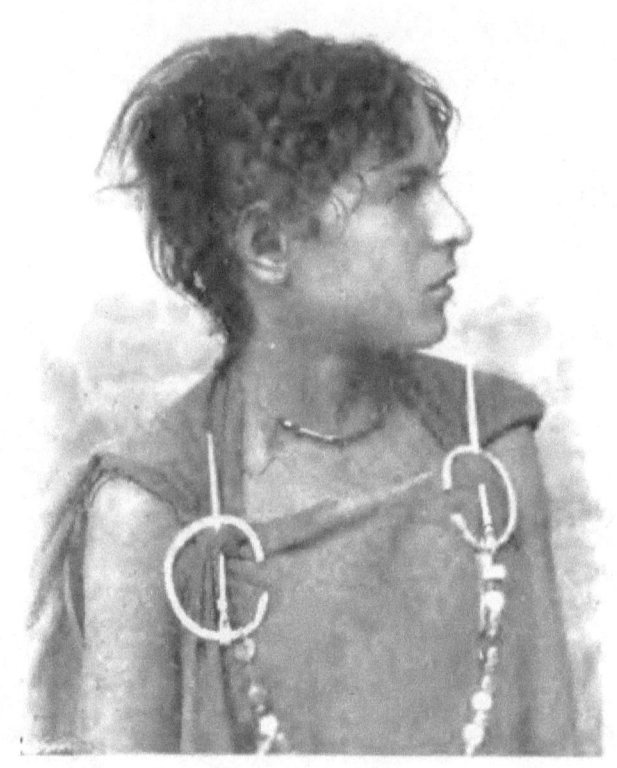

COUNTRY GIRL

and amber, and even the trouser buttons of French troopers. The men wear a woollen burnus over a cotton shirt, which they never change until it rots away. On their heads they have a great white turban wrapped round the ordinary red *sheshia*, and the tightness of the turban often deforms their heads in a grotesque manner. They either go barefoot or wear yellow sandals or woollen slippers with green leather soles.

ARAB COUNTRY WOMEN.

The Arabs of the Oases. The inhabitants of the oases have a bistre skin, thick lips, receding foreheads and chins. They appear to be descendants of white Berbers and Sudanese negroes. All round the oases are

TYPES OF WOMEN.

numerous tribes of nomadic Arabs, and, both in point of geography and population, the desert is gaining on the oases.

Costume. In the oases of the coast the men wear a brown woollen blouse and a little cloak.

COUNTRY WOMAN.

In the oases of the interior they wrap a long piece of brown woollen stuff round them like a toga. The women in each case wear the blue *peplos*, kept together with silver brooches.

Dwellings. Their dwellings are a poor imitation of those in the towns. You find stone villages, with the rooms opening into central court-yards. The various quarters of a village are generally separated by

COUNTRY WOMEN.

heavy gates, which are shut at night-fall; but sometimes there is merely a string hung across the road, and this is found nearly as effective.

Industries. The people of the oases are very hard-working, their chief occupation consisting in the irrigation of the various gardens, either by drawing water from wells, by an Artesian system dating back to pre-historic times, or by an elaborate arrangement of artificial streams. Carpets are made near Gabes and blankets at Gafsa, with archaic designs in which caravans, camels, crosses, gnomes, and fishes predominate.

One of the peculiar customs of the oases is that of eating dogs' flesh, although this was forbidden by the Koran. In extenuation of this, the natives plead that the meat is a wonderful specific against fever.

Troglodytes. The most interesting feature of the Southern districts of Tunisia consists in the strange dwellings, either handed down or imitated from prehistoric times. It is an excellent answer to the French, and other people who believe in modern progress, that it should have been found advantageous to revert to a kind of habitation which preceded the invention of houses. I have seen cave-dwellers in Eastern Spain; I believe there are still some in Japan and Mexico, and that an adaptation of the fashion survives at Bari and elsewhere; but there is certainly no other place in the world where the various kinds of troglodytes may all be observed so well within a narrow radius as in the South of Tunisia. Near Shnini the caves in the rocks have been taken as dwellings, just as Nature prepared them thousands of years ago. In neighbouring hillsides, the caves have been improved by scooping them out and providing them with rough masonry at the entrance. Hard by again, you may witness a third stage of development, the natives having found it less troublesome, and more in accordance with tradition, to scoop their dwellings out of the side of the rock rather than build houses with walls. The appearance of one of these villages, consisting of a succession of burrows beside each other along the face of a rock, is fanciful in the extreme, and suggests the abode of rabbits or prairie dogs rather than human beings.

The most perfect form of troglodyte dwelling is to be found in the Matmata plateau, and consists of underground rooms, passages and staircases excavated among the hills. Not only is it impossible to detect the troglodyte dwellings of the Matmatas from a distance, but even when you are among them you may often be unaware of their neighbourhood, and, making a careless step in a hole, may suddenly find yourself landed in the midst of a family party at supper. The soil is peculiarly adapted to this process, being at the same time soft enough for easy excavation and hard enough not to crumble away. The most curious feature about this collection of troglodyte dwellings is the rudimentary approach to them, which consists either of ledges or projecting stones, used as rough steps, which have been left in the original rock or else added in the form of masonry or wood-work. The troglodytes seem to possess the agility of monkeys, and it is an extraordinary sight to watch the men, and particularly the women, with huge burdens upon their backs, making their way up the sheer side of a cliff. They may also be observed on a fine day squatting and even sleeping upon these ledges at the entrance to their lairs. In the event of a disturbance, a rockful of cave-dwellers would be exceedingly difficult to dislodge from their natural fortifications; but as they are among the most peaceful and law-abiding of the

WOMAN OF OASIS OF GABES.

population, the French may safely be advised to leave them undisturbed, if only for the curiosity of this strange revival of the habits of prehistoric men.

The method of building in use among the troglodytes of the Matmatas is as follows: First of all a cubic space some thirty feet at the base is hewn out of the rock to make the patio or courtyard of the dwelling. When this is complete, the various other rooms are built with openings on to it, as in the case of all Arab houses, and a passage in the rock leads to the stables. At Shnini, among the Rhumeracen and elsewhere in the South, the natives remove all the soft rock which separates two calcareous strata on the side of a hill, and then proceed to build a stone frontage to the cavern thus hollowed out. In some of the troglodyte dwellings, when the excavation was made, pieces of the original rock were left inside, to form natural tables and beds and divans.

Perhaps one of the most extraordinary sights in the world is that of a lofty mountain of troglodyte dwellings standing out against the sky. The rock itself forms a natural fortress, with natural turrets and battlements, and is crenelated with the doorways of the dwellings which have been scooped out inside.

At Mednin we find the very last stage of troglodyte dwelling. It is no longer a cave, in any sense of the word, but its architecture is evidently modelled upon that of cave-dwellings scooped out of the side of the rock. It consists of a high, rugged wall with rude door-ways, dotted about above each other and beside each other in the most haphazard manner imaginable, and there are ledges of masonry for the inhabitants to clamber up into their hovels. Dwirat is perhaps the most striking and characteristic of the mountain-side troglodyte towns, and Tatawin is a village more or less troglodyte in its construction. But Shnini is the most mysterious of the troglodyte towns, having the appearance of a great white natural fortress from the outside. The inhabitants used to have close relations with the Tuaregs, and would no doubt continue to do so, but for the vigilance of the adjoining French garrison. The dialect of this region is much more nearly related to that of the Tuaregs than to any form of Arabic. Judging from the remains of Punic and Roman times remaining there, it must always have been a position of some importance, despite the inhospitable character of the district. So accurately have the troglodytes adapted their masonry to the character of the original rock, that it becomes a matter of great difficulty to distinguish the original from the artificial; and one may be pardoned for imagining that their dwellings have been in great part the work of Jinns.

The troglodytes are not the barbarians one might imagine them to be, judging merely by the elementary character of their houses. Not only do they have a number of primitive but ingenious home industries, but they are in considerable demand among the inhabitants of the whole Regency as cooks.

They are proud of their dwellings, which in many cases are exceedingly comfortable and furnished with some amount of luxury. They boast also that this is the natural form of dwelling, providing them as it does with the warmth of a Moorish bath in winter and the freshness of a well in the height of summer.

Home Life. The Arabs carry the patriarchal system to the utmost limits, the head of a family being an absolute master and, if he choose, an absolute tyrant. As a rule he takes his meals apart from the rest of the family, but sometimes he permits the presence of some of his elder sons. The women and younger children always have their meals afterwards, and with very little ceremony, contenting themselves with scraps and, oftener than not, eating them standing. When one of the sons is married, the bride is simply an additional member of the household, with no privacy, and no rights or privileges of her own. The servants, even when they are nominally free, occupy very much the same position as slaves used to do in the olden times. Their position, however, is not very different from that of other members of the family. No one receives wages or pocket money, but all expenses are provided by the head of the household, and every one is at his beck and call. It is interesting to compare the economy and organization of an Arab household with that of the Slav *zadruge*, which I have discussed in another work.

Harems. We in England are very fond of boasting about the Englishman's house being his castle, but it is more like a public-house if we compare it to the dwelling of a Muhammadan; and, though privacy is all very well in theory, it certainly has its drawbacks in practice when carried to such an extreme. As no officer of the law may violate a harem, there is obviously no safeguard for the life and liberty of its inmates. If any one disappears in a Muhammadan country, the harem system renders a search extremely difficult. An ill-disposed person has only to carry off his enemy into his house secretly, in order to keep him a prisoner for life, and even torture him or kill him. Mr. Marion Crawford founded a very exciting story, called "Paul Patoff," on this state of things, and none of his facts seem to have been in the least degree exaggerated. As there is practically no registration of births and deaths among the Muhammadans, murder is made all the more easy; and in any case there can be no difficulty in disposing of inconvenient bodies in a place which no stranger may enter.

Slavery, too, is an obvious result of the system. The whole civilized world has now spent its energies for the greater part of a century in trying to put down slavery; but all it has contrived to accomplish is a restriction of the public buying and selling of slaves. By resorting to fictitious marriages, and other subterfuges, the owner of a harem may procure as many slaves as he pleases, and once he has got them into his house, no one can possibly interfere to release them. Slaves can, of course, escape and claim protection from the Consulates, but, as a matter of fact, they are generally quite contented with their position, and know that such action could only involve them in ruin.

The harems of Tunis are much more difficult to visit than those of Turkey or Egypt, for the Tunisian Arabs are particularly strict about keeping their wives from contact with Europeans. Of course there is no great difficulty about visiting a poor harem through a guide, but you do not see there the beautiful carvings and costumes which are to be found in the more exclusive households. Mrs. Vivian was, however, fortunate enough, through the kindness of the wife of a French attaché, to see a particularly fine harem in the heart of the Arab quarter.

"We passed through heavy entrance gates," she says, "like those of a convent, and found ourselves in a small square, where we were confronted by a huge door, thickly studded with nails of all sorts of patterns and devices. Fatima's hand and the sign of the lyre are always introduced somewhere into the decoration, in order to ward off the evil eye. These doors are a great feature of Tunis houses, and many very beautiful specimens are to be seen in various parts of the town. A fat negress in gorgeous raiment opened to us, and we found ourselves in a big stone hall with long divans covered with matting. Here the men of the family sometimes sit, and it is the only place in the house where they may receive male visitors.

"Passing through, we came to a large patio, or open court-yard, where beautiful slender white marble columns harmonized exquisitely with dazzling white arabesques of infinitely delicate patterns, and walls covered with old tiles of many soothing colours. A little fountain was playing in the middle, and a pretty gazelle began to caper about at our approach. We were led straight up into the best bedroom, where we found our hostess clad in all her bravery and smiling on us with bland benevolence. She was a funny little fat stumpy woman, probably considered a great beauty in Tunisia. She had a round good-tempered face, a pink-and-white complexion not wholly guiltless of rouge, dark eyes touched up with kohl, and very scanty dark hair, parted in the middle and brushed most smoothly away under her cap and veil. She wore white silk trousers, and a short, loose coat of brilliant rose-coloured brocade embroidered in pink and silver. Her bright yellow, high-heeled shoes, elaborately worked in gold, were at least three sizes too small for her, and she hobbled about so painfully in them that we expected every moment to see her fall on her nose. Her little fat fingers were covered right down to the knuckles with rings. Of these she was evidently very proud, as she constantly spread out her hands for us to admire them. Various chains were hung round her neck, and she had an immense variety of brooches and other ornaments fastened into her dress and hair. She was probably about eighteen, but she looked five-and-thirty at least.

"She shook hands with us, and an attendant placed chairs for us opposite hers. It is considered terribly modern to use chairs in a harem, the usual habit being to squat cross-legged on cushions, or even on the floor, as was done in all the other rooms we entered. This was also the only room that possessed a table. In the others everything, from pickle-making to the fabrication of *kus-kus*, the national dish, was done on the floor. The best bed-room was comparatively tidy, but everywhere else I observed the most terrible confusion. Old Vichy water bottles were strewn about in all directions, and I had to walk warily to avoid knocking them over with my dress. The whole family seemed to be in a state of picnic, which I believe is the usual thing in Arab houses. On all hands, however, there were beautiful arabesque decorations and tiles. My friend praised them enthusiastically in French and by signs,—neither our host nor our hostess understood a word of anything but Arabic—but I was more cautious, knowing that Arabs generally dislike to have their possessions admired, and do not make allowances for European manners.

"It is considered particularly unlucky to admire children, as this is thought to expose them to the evil eye. There were some very pretty little girls playing about, but I am afraid that I must have distressed their parents very much by my admiration of them, as I did not remember that the correct thing to say was, '*Tabark Allah*,—may God preserve them from the evil eye.' When a really well-bred Arab goes to call on a friend, he says with a sweet smile, 'What a hole this is. Have you ever seen human beings live in such a tumble-down hovel before? It really isn't fit to put horses in.' Then the host is delighted, for he knows that his friend in his heart thinks everything charming, and that he is merely trying to keep the Jinns, or evil spirits, off the scent; as, if they heard the house being admired, they would certainly pounce down and do some harm.

"In Tunis you are always received in the best bedroom, which is invariably hung with bright butter-coloured brocade or satin. The rooms are shaped like a T upside down, and the furniture is always more or less alike. In each corner is an elaborately carved bed, sometimes entirely gilt, sometimes of black wood with a gigantic gilt 'Fatima's hand' above it, to protect the sleepers from the evil eye. In front is a small low bed where the children sleep. At the side of the bed stands a lofty grandfather's clock, which always seems to have stopped short never to go again. Beside each clock is a high mirror-wardrobe, thickly ornamented with ormolu. Facing each wardrobe is a chest of drawers with a marble top, on which is collected an amazing array of the most rubbishy artificial flowers under glass cases. It is further decorated with atrocious vases, such as would be scouted in the smallest English cottage, but which are considered in Tunis the very essence of fine art. The ceilings are beautifully painted and gilded, and round the upper part of the walls there are arabesques, forming a deep frieze. In this house the walls were laden with mirrors in elaborate gilt frames, which, our host proudly informed us, had come all the way from Belgium.

"The maid-servants, in their best clothes, stood round their mistress, staring at us, very curious, and vastly amused. Presently one of them brought in some thick Moorish coffee, which was excellent. My friend then asked our host if he would allow his wife to come and have tea with her one day, as she lived near. She promised not to let her husband or any other man come near the house all that afternoon; but the man was quite angry, and answered roughly 'No!' A Tunisian lady of high rank is never, under any circumstances, allowed to go out, as she would be in Turkey or Egypt. When she goes to her husband's palace in the country, a carriage is drawn into the courtyard, she gets in, and brightly coloured curtains are drawn tightly across each window. The carriage is then taken into the street, the mules are put in, and a guard mounts on the box. When she arrives at her destination, she is not allowed to alight until the carriage is safely inside the courtyard, and even then she sometimes has to veil. Many an Arab lady never leaves her house from the time she is married until she is carried out to be buried.

"A woman of the middle class is allowed more liberty, and occasionally goes out for walks, accompanied as a rule by a servant. The poor creature is enveloped in masses of white drapery, which make her look like a walking bundle, and in front of her face she arranges a large black scarf embroidered with red, blue, and white flowers. It falls to her knees, and, even by holding up the ends, she cannot see more than a foot or two of the road before her. I often wonder that she does not get run over when she goes out alone, for I am sure she needs a dog to guide her quite as much as any blind man. Servants and other women of the lower classes wear pieces of black crepon wound tightly round their faces, leaving just a slit for their eyes to peer through, and they are equally muffled up in white draperies. Seen from a distance, they might be men with masks or thick black beards, as in Arab countries it is by no means easy to tell a man from a woman at first sight. The older and uglier a woman is, the more prudish she seems to be about covering up her face, which, after all, is rather considerate on her part. Even the greater number of the negresses wear the yashmak, but the Bedouin women never do. Indeed, I am told that among the Tuaregs there is a tribe whose men wear veils and

MIDDLE-CLASS WOMAN AND SERVANT.

whose women go about with their faces uncovered. These are probably the 'New Women' of Africa.

"As may be imagined, a regular conversation was by no means easy with a hostess who spoke nothing but Arabic; so she occupied herself with a minute examination of our dresses. What she particularly enjoyed was pulling at my coat and investigating the embroidery upon it. Then the whole family would gather round me and pluck at my things, being especially interested in my long tortoiseshell eye-glasses. I came off very well, though, as they contented themselves with patting me gently, and discussing my raiment with each other. Some people are not so lucky, as I was told by an Englishman who lives in Tunisia. When the Duchess of Saxe-Coburg Gotha was in Tunis, she was very anxious to see a harem, so he arranged for her to visit the house of an old Arab friend of his. He said to the man, 'The lady who is coming to see you is the daughter of the Emperor of all the Russias, and has married the son of an English Queen.' The old man was too polite to show any incredulity; but when he saw a little lady dressed in ordinary European clothes he was quite convinced that he was being hoaxed. A great Princess, he said to himself, could not possibly go about except attended by a large suite and attired in brocade or cloth of gold. The Duchess came out of the house terribly dishevelled, for the women had pulled her hair about, taken the combs out of her hair to look at them, tugged at her dress to see how strong the material was, and even attempted to undo it to find out what she wore underneath. She was immensely amused, but declared that, now she had seen one harem, she was satisfied, and had no desire ever to visit another. Very many Tunisian women have never seen an European, so they are very curious about our clothes.

"When I was taken over the house, I noticed a great number of cages containing cheerful little singing birds, which are always a great feature of Tunisian houses. One small dark bird the Arabs are very fond of; they think it brings them luck, and call it the 'Father of Friends.'

"As in most Tunisian houses, the rooms were draped with yellow silk, the beds were gorgeously gilt, and the walls covered with mirrors in heavy gold frames. The kitchen was the most cheerful part of the house. There must have been nearly a dozen women bustling about preparing the evening meal. There were no stoves, but half a dozen little braziers were dotted about on the ground, while the cook squatted down beside them to arrange the food. Big heaps of vegetables and vivid scarlet chillies were scattered about to be used for the *kuskus*, and bowls of bright-coloured sauces were being mixed for it. Needless to say, all the preparations were made on the ground.

"A rich Arab's wife leads a very lazy sort of life. She has absolutely no education, and leaves the management of her house to servants, though it sometimes amuses her to do a little cooking. Her day is usually taken up with bathing, dressing, and sleeping. There are bands of negresses, who go round the harems dancing and playing on two-stringed instruments, tambourines and castanets, or singing in harsh, cracked voices. Some of these negresses are lively and entertaining, and are in great request as story-tellers.

"A great Arab lady is never allowed to see a man

if it is possible to avoid it; or, rather, he is not allowed to see her, for she manages to catch sight of people, even through her double lattices of wood and iron. Her brother may only visit her with her husband's permission. When she is ill, and it is absolutely imperative that a doctor should be sent for, great are the preparations. A servant has to be in attendance and hides her completely under the bed clothes. Supposing that her pulse has to be felt, then the servant covers her hand and arm so carefully that only the wrist is visible. If she has hurt her back, a hole is made in the sheets so that the doctor may just be able to see the injured place. If he insists upon seeing her tongue, the precautions are still more elaborate, and the attendant covers her face with both hands, just leaving room between the fingers that she may put out her tongue.

"We may come away from harems with sentiments of pity for the prisoners, but they themselves are quite content. Strangely enough, it is the women who are most against any reform. They look on Europeans with horror and sometimes with amazement; and I think it will be long before the New Woman makes her appearance in Tunisian harems."

Vulgarizing by Civilization. One of the worst results of the French occupation is the influence upon native costumes and native art, which will certainly die away before very long. Every lady who visits a harem tells you that the inmates take the greatest pride in any trumpery European clothes or ornaments which they may have contrived to secure, and think nothing of their own beautiful native handiworks. A missionary lady told me that very often an Arab woman of the country districts would show her with great glee an hideous and objectionable picture of an European dancing woman, or other professional beauty, taken from a half-penny paper or the cover of a chocolate box, exclaiming, "You will like to see this. Here is a picture of a Christian woman. Is it not beautiful? Whenever I look at it I shall be reminded of you." When the missionary derided the work of art, there was great consternation, and the natives would shuffle it away sorrowfully, saying, with tears in their eyes, that they would never look at it again. I shall never forget the expression of bewilderment on the face of an Arab woman when a missionary lady, supposed to be making a mere visit of ceremony, suddenly embarked upon an harangue about pureness of heart. I remonstrated with the lady afterwards, and told her that she would have done much better to leave these people alone to the enjoyment of a religion which did far more than Christianity does in Europe to keep people straight. She admitted with some reluctance that Muhammadanism had many good points, but presently she turned up the whites of her eyes and remarked with unctuous fanaticism, "Alas! poor people, their condition is pitiable, for they have no knowledge of salvation!"

Women's Rights. She assured me that the spiritual position of the women in the interior is worse than that of the men, a Muhammadan being by no means sure that a woman possesses a soul. She added that the women rarely trouble to say their prayers, and, more important still, that they do not consider themselves bound so completely by the ordinances of cleanliness. This would be regrettable, for they must, like all women, have a great deal to say to the rearing of male children, who will be influenced by the ideas of their mothers even though they may be taught to consider them of little or no account. But I am told that this is after all not the case, and that the women observe the ordinances of religion more strictly than the men. Also that a woman has great power in the house. It is said that, if the husband finds his wife's shoes outside the door of her room, he does not dare to enter.

I could not help being interested by the difference in consideration paid, by women as well as men, to children according to their sex. The landlady of my hotel at Kairwân had a native nurse for her little boy, and told me, as I could see for myself, that the woman was its most abject slave; but she added that, had it been a girl, it would probably have been left to its own devices, and would have received scarcely any attention at all.

Marriage. Those who grumble about marriages of convenience with us had better not become Moslems. It is rare with them that the bridegroom sees the bride until the actual wedding day. Some interpreters of the Koran say that a young man, who is likely to be accepted, may be allowed a glimpse of his future wife's face and the palms of her hands,—the latter evidently that he may judge her character and future by palmistry. But most Moslem bachelors have to trust to go-betweens or parents. Either the mother visits friends' harems and chooses a bride according to her taste, or fathers put their heads together and make up a match according to their interests, or else the young man relies upon a professional match-maker. He explains to her exactly what he wants, often in the words of an old Arab song, which says, " She must be not too fat and not too thin, she must have the black eyes of a gazelle, cheeks like masses of roses, a neck like an antelope . . and her tongue must not be too long."

Only in two cases can he know his future wife by sight: she may be either a relation or a slave. As several branches of a family often live together, cousins of both sexes are brought up in each other's society until they are nearly old enough to be married. It is not, therefore, surprising that young men, when called upon to marry, should remember the friends of their childhood and prefer them to strangers. " Marry strangers," says the Koran, but the advice is not always followed, and there is a popular saying that " He is a fool who marries a stranger when his cousin awaits him."

As to the other method of acquaintance, it will no doubt surprise a good many people to hear how largely slavery still exists even in civilized countries. Not only in Turkey, but in Algeria and Tunis under the French flag, even in Egypt under our own, very many harems are still recruited by means of the slave trade. When a man wants slaves nowadays, he does not send traders or raiders to Uganda, but he applies to some well-known purveyor in Constantinople or Asia Minor, a marriage contract is drawn up, and all the ceremonies of legal wedlock are gone through. The women thus obtained are nominally wives, but in reality slaves. They are bought for money, they are not consulted about the sale, and they cannot go away if they are discontented.

The ceremony of an Arab marriage is a lengthy affair, often lasting a whole week. When a match has been decided upon, there is a good deal of bargaining as to the dowry which shall be paid. The girl's father talks of selling her for a certain sum, but this is only a relic of old fashions, for the dowry is strictly tied up, and the wife alone can touch it or bequeath it. When the price has been fixed, the man sends all sorts of presents: henna to stain her nails red, paint for her face, scents, five-branched candles to avert the evil eye, dried fruits, embroidered shoes, and a gold coin to pay the woman who dresses her on her wedding day. If he means to be very attentive, he adds flowers, and even poetry of his own composition. Such is the extent of the Oriental imagination, that he often persuades himself he is seriously in love with a girl he has never seen. The girl's only contribution to the new household is a certain number of mules laden with silk stuffs and gilt furniture. It is a frequent sight in Arab towns to behold a procession of these mules, accompanied by the young men of the bride's family, wearing branches of jasmine over their ears. Her father gives her no other dowry, but she takes her share of the family inheritance after his death. The day before the wedding, the bridegroom goes to the steam bath and gives a banquet to his friends, while the bride has her nails stained, her eyebrows blackened, and her cheeks painted by her friends. Then she is brought with much ceremony to her new home, where there is feasting during many days. Lambs are roasted whole, and large quantities of coffee and sherbet are consumed. Public dancers are hired, and there is an incessant beating of drums, clashing of cymbals, and twanging of mandolines.

I saw in one village of Tunisia a very unhappy young woman, who was said to be sixteen years of age, but looked at least thirty according to our notions. She had been married six months before and divorced within two months of her wedding, whereupon she had simply returned to her father's house and resumed her old life there; but she had lost much of the consideration of her relations and neighbours. This sort of thing, I was told, is by no means uncommon, the cause of it usually being the difficulty of getting on with the husband's various female relations, who all live under one roof. A woman may succeed in satisfying her husband, but she has to be specially accommodating in order to find complete favour in the eyes of her mother-in-law and her husband's sisters and aunts.

Divorce. In theory, either husband or wife may divorce the other by a simple formality, without assigning any reason. In practice, a man can only divorce his wife if she is agreeable to it, or has been intolerably disagreeable to him. Sometimes they are divorced once or twice and then come together again. There exists a peculiarly solemn form of divorce, by which a man is debarred from marrying his wife again unless she first marries some one else and is divorced by him. In cases of necessity this second divorce is sometimes arranged, as a pure formality, by the intervention of a common friend. It might not be thought that this contingency would often arise, but the Arabs have a special word, *mustahal*, to describe the man who performs this strange service.

Funerals. One of the strangest and most affecting sights in an Arab town is that of the funerals, which may be met at any street corner. The corpse is merely wrapped in a mat of esparto grass, and carried either on a bier or on men's shoulders. The mourners lounge along, some in front and some behind, crooning verses of the Koran in melancholy tones, which haunt you for days afterwards. This wailing is, however, nothing to that which goes on in the house of the deceased. When I was staying in the country near Tunis, I heard it kept up during a whole night in a neighbouring village, and I can conceive nothing more desperately depressing than these strains of lamentation, wafted through the darkness by the breeze. My host's dog stood it less well even than I did, and felt constrained to join in the mournful chorus, until we were half tempted to put a bullet through its head.

Perhaps the strangest of all the funerals I saw was at Bizerta. It was that of a baby, which was being carried to its grave in an esparto basket. In Mrs. Vivian's photograph on page 233 the funeral procession is being conveyed across the harbour by the steam ferry. The basket containing the corpse is on the extreme right. The mourners were few, but they made up for their lack of number by the vehemence of their wails.

AN ARAB FUNERAL.

Food. The Beduins are content to subsist largely upon whatever nature may offer them. Roast locusts, acacia gums, and the coarse fruit of the jujube tree are among their favourite delicacies. *Kus-kus* is their staple food, consisting of fine meal boiled with mutton and strongly spiced. On grand occasions they spit a sheep or a lamb with a piece of wood and roast it slowly by turning it over the embers of a wood fire. It is then excellent eating, and travellers who receive it as tribute on their passage may consider themselves lucky. Like the Turks, the Beduins also indulge in little squares of boiled meat, to which they are in the habit of adding a sauce of rancid oil, without which they consider all meat to be tasteless. If you give any one of them the remains of a chicken, or any other food which has been cooked after the European fashion, they will consider it uneatable until it shall have received the addition of their own particular flavouring. One of their most characteristic dishes is the *shekshuka*, a mixture of every sort of vegetable—beans, potatoes, onions, wild thistles—and whatever spices they can afford. Oranges and dates are often added also to the mixture. Their pastry and sweetmeats are creations of considerable skill, but do not appeal to the European by reason of the rancid oil which can never be excluded altogether. As a great treat, camel's hump or fore-quarter of gazelle are sometimes provided. Mention must also be made of *meltsus*, pounded barley cooked with spices or honey or milk; *messelli*, salt meat dried in the sun; *kaadid*, meat preserved in oil; and *tebikha*, a mixture of green vegetables also saturated in oil. What most strikes an European about Arab cookery is the surprising mixture of sweets and savouries, or perhaps I should rather say unsavouries. The bread is generally made of semolina, and is very heavy, hardly anything in the nature of yeast being used. The beverages are restricted to water, milk, coffee, syrups, and a sweet decoction of flour, beside the palm wine, which is not drunk in its fermented condition by any but very lax Moslems. Tea is practically unknown. In the towns, a favourite dainty is a sweet fritter cooked in oil, very appetising to look upon but disgusting to the taste. In almost any street you may encounter boys hawking about platterfuls of this dainty, which is bought up with the utmost eagerness. All day and all night in Tunis you may hear the musical cry of "*Kakawia, Kakawia!*" (roast monkey-nuts), which the Arabs nibble at every spare moment.

Water-Drinking. No one can travel among the Arabs without being struck by the importance attached to the water supply. Where a rich Englishman would bequeath money to founding a hospital or decorating a church, an Arab can think of no other channel for his charity than the construction of a fountain, which will assure him the blessings of all future generations. This is his one idea of good works, and it is worth noting that every mosque or shrine has generous supplies of water attached to it. The Arabs have a curious characteristic in common with horses and many other animals. They prefer stagnant water, however disgusting in smell and appearance, to the most limpid running water, which they assert generally contains disagreeable medicinal properties. Whenever they are reduced to drinking running water in remote places, it always disagrees with them, and often makes them sick; but this may be in a great measure due to habit and prejudice transmitted through many generations.

A strict Muhammadan refrains not only from wine but from tobacco. In the towns, the Moors nearly all smoke, but in the country districts the Arabs generally content themselves with taking snuff, to the manufacture of which the greater part of the tobacco grown in Tunisia is devoted.

Drugs. Moslems are forbidden to drink wines or spirits, but in Tunis they contrive to reach the same ends by smoking preparations of hemp. The milder kind is called *kif*, which is prepared from the flowers, and if used in moderation has no more effect than wine; but the concentrated essence, known as *shira*, or hashish, produces intoxication as quickly as raw spirits, and leads to delirium tremens. The dangerous part of this habit is that, once acquired, it is very difficult to throw off. Its devotees are amongst the greatest sufferers from the enforced abstinence of Ramadan.

Bang is a ruder preparation of hemp, generally taken in the form of pills mixed with opium, but the use of this is commoner further East. A friend of mine, travelling in India, had an admirable servant who, after some days' journey in a remote part of the interior, suddenly collapsed, and could neither work nor walk. Various remedies were tried, but in vain, and at last he was induced to confess that his provision of bang had come to an end, and that he could not possibly recover until he obtained a fresh supply, which had to be sent for from a distance of many days' journey. The consumption of hashish is nominally forbidden in Tunisia, but goes on everywhere. If you enter almost any coffee-house in Tunis, and offer to pay a few pence for a pipeful, the host will at once produce a kind of gourd-shaped bulb with a long stem, fill it with hashish, light it with a few strong puffs, and hand it round to the company. If they are unaccustomed to it, the only result will be to make them cough until they nearly choke. If taken seriously, however, it often has the strangest effects, giving all kinds of wild ideas and exaggerating the simplest sensations. Two Englishmen, who visited a hashish den in Tunis, told me that they found long rows of men squatting round the walls buried in thought and silence. Their guide told them that it might be dangerous to disturb the smokers, and led them off to a far corner, where they were provided with pipes. One of them was seized with the idea that he was kept down by a great weight, and it took several hours before he could be persuaded to get up and go home. The other did nothing but laugh stupidly, and developed a mania for roaming. He had to be chased half round the Arab quarter before he could be taken back to his hotel, and on arriving there, he developed a tendency to roam into other people's rooms. Hashish induces a kind of temporary lunacy, with sensations which are sometimes highly agreeable, and sometimes very much the reverse.

The Arabs of Tunis give their children a great deal of opium, to prevent their crying. It has been calculated that each child consumes on an average an infusion of one poppy-head every evening of his life up to the age of two years. Yet he seems to thrive on it.

Of Learning Arabic. Beginners are often alarmed by the strangeness of the Arab as of the Russian character.

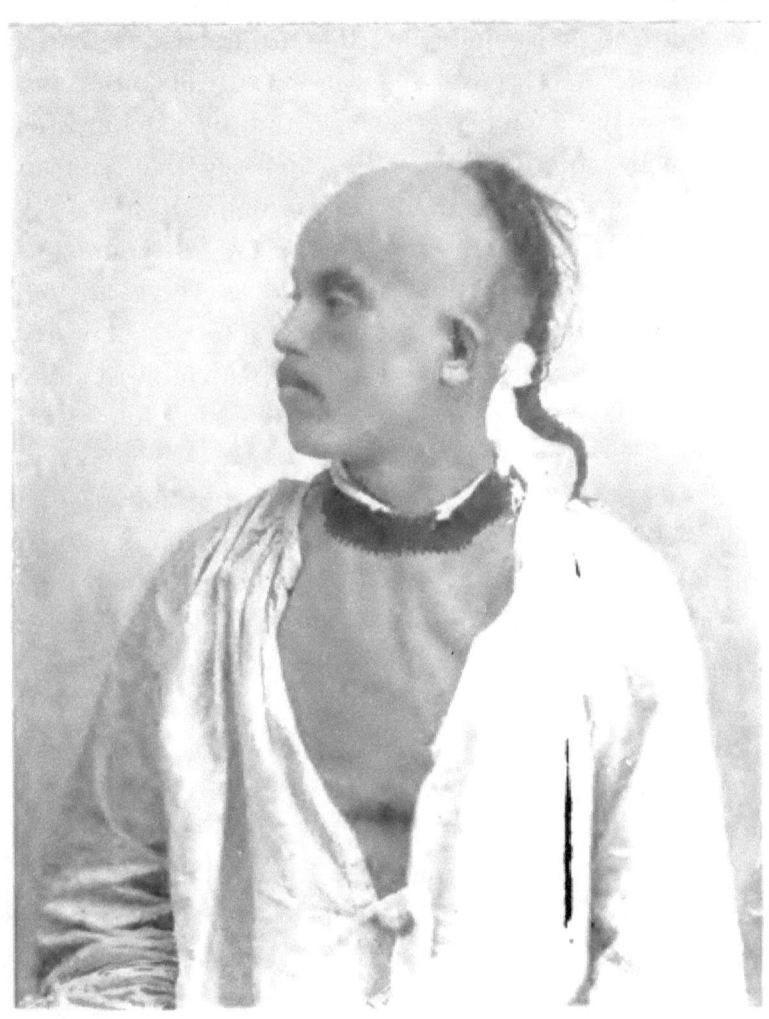

AFTER BLOODLETTING.

But the Russian may be learned in a few hours, and the Arab character by a few days' application. Some sounds are hard to pronounce, particularly by French throats, but Germans soon master them, and the British have no cause for despair. My teacher told me with pride how he enabled a French officer to circumvent the guttural k by inducing him to practise it with a paper-knife laid across his tongue. Still more perplexing is the gasping letter *'ain*, and my teacher often exclaimed impatiently: "Try to fancy that you are being sea-sick—thus shall you accomplish it easily."

For all difficulties there is, however, full compensation in the charming turns of phrase which a study of Arabic reveals to the astonished student. He may express as much as Lord Burleigh with almost equal brevity. Is a beggar importunate, the sole word "*Iftah*" is understood to mean, "May Allah open to thee the gates of good, for I have nothing to give thee." Does an unwelcome stranger enter, it is enough to look up and sourly exclaim, "*Bismillah!*"—the expression used at every hour of the day as an incantation against evil spirits—and your intruder will understand you to mean, "Who is this ugly Jinn come hither to torment us?" Does a merchant in the bazaars fix a monstrous price, the correct course is to raise the hands towards heaven and ejaculate: "There is neither strength nor power save in Allah, the high, the great, the Master of Worlds." The merchant will not fail to understand that his price has seemed to surpass all human possibilities. Other pious phrases have sometimes a humorous turn. Thus you may tell a merchant: "*Inshallah* (if it please Allah), I will return and buy another day," but you and he know full well that the pleasure of Allah will not bring this about.

Arabic scholars, who come from Syria, or even Egypt, have considerable difficulty in making themselves understood, and are often tempted to vow impatiently that the Tunisians cannot be real Arabs at all, but must be some mongrel Berber race. There is also a marked difference between the accent of Tunisia and that of Algeria, still more of Morocco, but it is a difference not in the construction of the language so much as in the use of distinct words which are understood all over Tunisia but nowhere else. Classical Arabic is of course intelligible only to the learned, and would be of very little assistance to a traveller in asking his way.

Greetings. As a general rule, particularly in the town of Tunis, where few people are fanatical, it is safe to use the ordinary salutation, "*Selam a'alek*, the peace (of Allah and his Prophet) be with thee"; but a very strict Moslem may resent it and think to himself, "Who is this infidel dog, who ventures to offer me blessings from Allah and the Prophet, in whom he does not believe?" Nor will he himself waste such blessings upon an infidel. But the Arabic language is so very rich in salutations and compliments that he need be at no loss to find plenty which will not hurt his conscience to use or to accept. Beside the usual compliments of the time of day, every sort of inquiry about your health and the health of all your family is customary on the part of an Arab. When two Arabs meet in the street or elsewhere after a long separation, there seems no end to the string of inquiries which they exchange. Even half an hour of this occupation is thought nothing of. "How are you?" "How is your health?" "How is your father?" "How are your other relations?" — each being enumerated separately, even the most distant ones. "How is your household?" "How are your men?" "Are you well?" "Is nothing wrong with you?" "Do you lack nothing?" And so on. It is considered bad form to inquire after female relations directly, but they are generally included in such terms as "household," or "family." When a man's ingenuity is at last exhausted, and the various questions have all been answered satisfactorily, it is considered a great compliment to make sure of the reality of your good health by asking all the same questions over again and awaiting the answers with equal anxiety. This process may be repeated an indefinite number of times according to the effusiveness of the speaker. When at last one man has completed his inquiries, it is the turn of the other, who will be thought exceedingly ungracious if he be behindhand in the number of his questions. The answers are generally prefaced by the words *elhamdou lillah* (thanks be to Him, that is, Allah), and they often contain elaborate compliments, such as "I have lacked nothing save to behold the light of thy countenance and the length of thy days."

Curses.
The vocabulary of abuse is no less rich, and very little is thought of such amenities as "May Allah curse thy parents"; "May the sea pass over thee", "Allah grant that thou mayest

go to bed and never rise again." A severe insult is to call a man "*boujadi*," which means little more than an ignorant or ill-bred person; and it is curious to notice that among the Tuscans there is nothing more offensive than to call a man *ignorante*, which conveys the same imputation upon his breeding. Similarly, the Spaniards resent nothing so much as to be called "*sin verguenza*" (without shame). The Arabs are also fond of causing annoyance by casting imputations upon the morality of a man's parents, but the greatest insult of all is to call an Arab a Jew. It is not so very long ago that any one who did this was liable to be given in charge of the nearest policeman and sentenced straightway to the bastinado.

Proverbs. It is impossible to give in a short space any real idea of the wit and wisdom embodied in Tunisian proverbs, but a few may be cited, though I cannot guarantee that any of them belong exclusively to the Regency. At any rate, it has given me a certain amount of pleasure to make the collection.

"He who desires to attain to great things must pass through many nights."

"He who has gold is beloved, though he be a dog, and the son of a dog."

"Shun him who can be of no use to thee: in this world he cannot serve thee, and in that which is to come he cannot intercede on thy behalf."

"It is better to commit ten sins in the sight of God than one in the sight of men."

"Those who are learning to shave heads practise upon those of orphans."

"To the dog who has money men say, 'My lord dog.'"

"The man who spends the night in a marsh wakes up a cousin to the frogs."

"Good morrow, neighbour, let us remain, I in my house and thou in thine."

"The beauty of a man lies in his intelligence: the intelligence of a woman is to be found in her beauty."

"When the moon is with thee, of what account are the stars?"

"Every beetle in his mother's eyes is a gazelle."

"When thou seest two people in constant converse, thou mayest know that the one is the dupe of the other."

"Better a bad prince than protracted democracy."

"Obedience to women is the avenue of hell."

"Consult thy wife, and do the reverse of what she advises."

"Joy lasts for seven days, but sadness endures for a life-time."

Chapter IV

ISLAM

Conversion to Islam—Mosques—Graveyards—Ramadan—Bairam—Drunken Moslems—Photography—The Aïssawas—Shrines and Seers—The Merabut of Baghdad—The Story of a Jinn—Amulets—Fortune-tellers.

When I wrote a book about Servia, I naturally devoted some attention to the religious ceremonies, which are always the most picturesque aspect of a people; and one of my critics reproached me with describing, in a book upon Servia, incidents which are common to all branches of the Orthodox Church. Still less will he probably acquiesce in my dealing here with the great religion, which is broadly the same throughout the whole Muhammadan world. But the duty of any one who seeks to describe a country is, methinks, to present it as it strikes him, and as it will strike others who follow in his footsteps. No doubt it would require many volumes to do justice to Islam, but an account of Tunis which ignored Islam altogether would be a salad without the dressing. I must therefore frankly crave indulgence, and confess that this chapter seeks only to pourtray those outlines and salient points of the Muhammadan religion which are most likely to arouse the intelligent curiosity of a traveller in Tunisia.

Conversion to Islam. My teacher of Arabic told me that it was a matter of the utmost ease to embrace Islam; and, though he was neither fanatical nor even religious, he never tired of trying to persuade me to do so. "It is only a matter of about half an hour," he would say to me; "you have only to come with me and make a declaration before the religious authorities that there is but one God and that Muhammad is His prophet. Then if you will give up wearing a hat, be circumcised, observe Ramadan, pray and make ablutions regularly, you will be as good a Muhammadan as any of us." I said I drew the line at circumcision, but he replied that, if I would obtain a medical certificate that it would be dangerous to my health, the formality would probably be dispensed with. On the other hand, he warned me that the religious authorities would remark to me that, if I were really a true believer, I ought to be prepared to make this small sacrifice for my creed. There are really no dispensations in Islam, he told me. It is a democratic religion wherein all believers are equal. Every Moslem is in direct relation with God and needs the intervention of no priest. The Muhammadan clergy are merely the most diligent among the worshippers, and neither undergo consecration nor acquire any greater authority than is conferred upon them by their reputation. Not even the Sultan, whom all true Moslems recognise as the head of their religion, can dispense any one of them from the most trifling duty.

The great inducement which my teacher held out was that, once I had accepted Islam, I should be free to visit all the mosques, and even undertake the pilgrimage to the holy cities. A document would be given me, setting forth that I had been received into the faith, and, if I produced this, no one, however fanatical, would be able to make any objection to me even at Mecca. Indeed, it would rarely be necessary even to produce this document, for every one would be satisfied by my merely repeating the formula of Islam. Of course, if I went out of mere curiosity and came into collision with any prejudices, by taking photographs or by any other indiscretion, I might get into trouble; but with a few elementary precautions I should be perfectly safe anywhere. It would be quite unnecessary for me to attempt, as Burton did, to conceal the fact that I was an European. Indeed, I am assured on many hands that the difficulties of a pilgrimage to Mecca have been absurdly exaggerated by travellers in order to enhance the importance of their exploits. Burton, for instance, looked every inch an Oriental, and needed no elaborate disguise to conceal his European origin, apart from the fact that in his day there was no distrust of European visitors. Nowadays, more especially since a foolish anti-Turkish prejudice has been propagated in Europe, a visit to Mecca might be attended with danger and difficulties; but these would not be insuperable by any one who possessed the most rudimentary notions of how to behave.

Mosques. It is a source of regret to the traveller that he should be excluded from the mosques of Tunis, and, though he has access to those in the holy city of Kairwán, which are much finer, he will always imagine he has missed a spectacle. At the outset of the occupation, the French announced that they would respect the mosques of any town which freely opened its gates to them. Kairwán kept her gates closed for a brief space, and as a kind of protest; so the French general seized the pretext and rode straight into the yard of the chief mosque, an event which produced, as it was intended to produce, a profound impression throughout the country. Since this the mosques of Kairwán have remained accessible to all men. This was also the case at Sfax, but a French soldier having provoked a disturbance in one of the mosques there some time later, the old privilege was restored in compensation. Many French people think it would be wiser to insist on admittance to all the mosques, but this would arouse widespread discontent among the natives. It is difficult to understand why Moslems, who proselytize so ardently, should be so jealous of the presence of strangers at their devotions. I can appreciate an objection to the treading of prayer carpets by dirty boots, or to the disturbance of meditation by talkers and walkers, but that is a ground for regulation rather than for exclusion.

Graveyards. The graveyards of Tunisia, just as much as the mosques there, are forbidden ground to Infidels. In Algeria, however, you may wander where you will; and there are often picturesque scenes in the Muhammadan cemeteries there, particularly at the tomb of a *merabut*, or Moslem saint, where pilgrims come to pay their devotions. The saint's tomb is draped with rich prayer-carpets and hangings, and is flanked by an array of flags surmounted by crescents. Lanterns are sometimes lit there during the nights of Ramadan, and give a weird, ghostly effect to the cemeteries. The flags and draperies are votive offerings, put up on much the same principle as the ornaments hung by pious Papists on the altars of their saints. A man is in trouble, or desires something, and he makes a vow that, if everything goes right, he will place a flag at the tomb of a certain *merabut*. Then, from time to time, he will come to offer prayers or recite passages of the Koran at this sacred spot.

At the entrance to the tomb may be noticed the shoes which the pilgrims have doffed before venturing on holy ground. The little white chapels are also receptacles for votive offerings. Some deposit incense, others light fairy-lamps there, others bring candles, oil, and various negotiable articles. A certain *merabut* is supposed to have a particular fancy for olives, another for sheep-skins. Such is the extent of this practice that there was recently a law-suit at Tunis, between two branches of a *merabut's* family, as to which of them should be entitled to carry off the

ISLAM

offerings. The invocation of saints is entirely contrary to the spirit and teaching of Islam, but it has made great strides of late. Madness is considered a proof of saintliness by Muhammadans, and many of their most venerated *merabuts* would with us have been shut up in asylums. They have even borrowed some of their *merabuts* from the Christians. They venerate Cardinal Lavigerie as " the Scarlet Merabut." and S. Louis as " Sidi Bu Said." They have a legend that S. Louis became a Moslem before he died.

Ramadan. The great Muhammadan fast lasts every day from the boom of a cannon at 4 a.m. to the boom of a cannon at sunset. It is said that the first ten days go like a horse's gallop, the next ten like the trot of a mule, and the last ten days like the amble of an ass. Every day men's tempers grow shorter, they are less patient when a carriage jostles them in the streets, and their latent fanaticism finds easier vent. To the stranger, Ramadan is the pleasantest time for visiting a Moslem country. He is under no obligation to fast, though he will safeguard susceptibilities if he abstain from smoking in the Arab quarter, as a native who inhaled a passing puff from a cigar by accident would be held to have broken the fast, and this would entail an extra day's penance in the following month.

The visitor may regret the closing of all the coffee-houses during the day, but ample amends are made to him by the recurrence of a nightly carnival, where simple Oriental gaiety is allowed full swing. Fairy lamps are lit round every minaret; there are merry-go-rounds and marionettes for the children; that sad dog Karagus, an Arab punchinello, is exhibited by means of Chinese shadows for those who like strong meat; and in every coffee-house, down to the remotest limits of the Arab quarters, are deafening musicians with barbaric instruments, pantomime dances, reverend story-tellers devising supplements to the Arabian Nights, or droll travesties of familiar beasts. The correct thing is to lounge from show to show, carrying a provision of strange sweetmeats compounded of honey and oil, or filling the pockets with roast peas and pumpkin seeds to chew as a pastime.

Ramadan lasts only a lunar month, but it is observed far more strictly than the forty days in Roman Catholic or even in Orthodox countries. Imagine the hardship, particularly in a hot country, of not being allowed to eat a single morsel or drink a drop of any liquid between the small hours and sunset. Moslem fasters have an advantage, however, over the Christians, in that they are permitted to eat, drink, and be merry during the night-time to the full extent of their inclination after a long day's abstinence. The amusements, which go on during the nights of Ramadan, are practically the same as those of Bairam, the three days of carnival that follow. They are, perhaps, more picturesque, owing to the passion for illumination; and I confess I know no more enchanting sight than that of an Eastern city with all the mosques and minarets and most of the principal houses deco-

ISLAM

rated with rows of fairy-lights. But there is certainly more go and vigour of enjoyment when Ramadan is over and there is no more fasting to be done for another year.

Without spending Ramadan among the Arabs, it

NEGRO BOGEY MAN DANCING IN BAIRAM.
(*Photograph by Mrs. Vivian.*)

is impossible to obtain the faintest insight into the character of a people whose lightest thoughts and actions belong to the realms of poetry.

Bairam. The three days following Ramadan are known as Bairam, and constitute one of the chief festivals of the Moslems, who, not content with writing backwards, place their Lent before their carnival. In 1898, the first and greatest day of Bairam coincided with the last and greatest day of the

JEWISH DANCING-GIRL.

Roumi carnival, so the town was doubly alive. Tawdry cars were competing for banners, and paper confetti were being flung about the French boulevards, while the square and street of Halfawine gave themselves up to the picturesqueness of Oriental gaiety. Old-fashioned croakers complained that the illuminations by night and the fun by day were not what they used to be, but they must ever remain a real delight.

The marionettes were wonderfully quaint. I recall most particularly an exquisitely hideous lion, whose jaws snapped ferociously every time a string was pulled. There were strange dances, performed in tents by Jews, for a Moslem deems it beneath his dignity to dance or to sing; a man standing in a doorway clapped his hands with vast solemnity as he invited all and sundry to visit his show; strolling minstrels beat barbaric tom-toms, and promenaded their bagpipes in fair imitation of the true Scottish style. But perhaps the show which most delighted me was one exhibited in a kind of stable. The audience squatted round the walls while the performers dressed themselves up as various familiar animals, and pranced about most drolly in the centre. There was an ostrich, whose particular joke it was to stretch out a long red flannel neck and nibble at your face. The camel was also very witty; but the horse, draped in patch-work chintz, out of which the rider's body emerged, afforded most delight of all. As he pranced more fantastically and more wildly, the enthusiasm of the audience kept on increasing, and I went away marvelling how completely and how easily I had been amused.

All along the streets was a dense crowd of loungers, clad in their newest and brightest raiment. The Arabs wear cloaks of many colours at all times, but Bairam seems to be the occasion for replenishing their wardrobes, and each donned new, resplendent vesture. None so humble but he contrived to afford a new cloak or new shoes for Bairam. Free play was

BOYS IN BEST CLOTHES AT BAIRAM.
(*Photograph by Mrs. Vivian.*)

accorded to fancy, and even the most uproarious combinations of magenta, orange, and sky-blue seemed always in exquisite taste. Men wore massive silver rings on their fingers, and even in their ears, over which, like clerk's pencils, they hung favours of coloured paper or little bouquets made to imitate rosettes.

It was, perhaps, more than anything a children's

BAIRAM: SWINGS.
(Photograph by M. N.)

heyday. Here was a swing holding a dozen youngsters, all shouting at the top of their voices, while the conductor yelled an antiphon as he propelled his charges with ever-increasing vigour. Next to the swings, the chief delight of the young Arabs was to ride about the town, either two on a diminutive donkey or a dozen in an *araba*, clad in vivid vesture and roaring from sheer lightness of heart.

And then the stalls! Even the pop-guns and tin swords, obviously made in Germany, acquired an Oriental interest from the fantasy of their arrangement; and the fruit booths were works of art. Mountains of nuts and oranges were sold, and there were tumblers of white sherbet for throats parched by constant shouting. The coffee-houses, whose hermetic blue shutters had been up all day during so many weeks, were once more smiling and thronged; long rows of white-robed figures sat cross-legged and blinked serenely over their coffee-cups at the hubbub all around. They, rather than the younger revellers, symbolized the contemplative spirit of Islam. With their vast treasures of imagination, which far exceed anything Aryan, their Paradise lay within. The silence, and the strength, and the majesty of Islam,— how they were brought home to us at every turn. What stored dignity was expressed in the ceremonial greetings of Bairam. Every acquaintance was met with a patriarchal embrace, a kiss on the shoulder, a hand on the heart, and the humblest kissing the fingers with which they had touched the bernus of a venerated Sheikh. To return from these inspiring visions to the horseplay of the Frank carnival, the chintz dominoes, the garish cars, was like a rude awakening from a beautiful dream.

The consumption of alcohol by the natives has been

ISLAM

largely on the increase since the French occupation.

Drunken Moslems. During the Bairam festivities, I saw drunken Moslems reeling about the streets far into the night. The Bey's police were busy hustling these offenders off to the cells, where in old days they would have been bastinadoed, but where they now merely suffer a short imprisonment. Similar reduction has been applied to the punishment for breaking the Fast of Ramadan. The French wished to abrogate this latter penalty, but the Bey stood firm, declaring that the matter concerned his people and his religion.

Doubtless many Moslems do break the Fast, but they cannot do so easily, as public opinion is strong on the matter, especially among the women, and the only chance of obtaining food would be by slinking into a French café, where they might easily be observed. Perhaps public opinion does not reprobate strong drink quite so sternly as breaking Ramadan, and absinthe or anisette are often excused with the old quibble that, as they were unknown in the days of the Prophet, he could not have forbidden them. Despite the sturdy conservatism of Islam, it is to be observed with regret that many venerable uses are dying out. Yet a little while, and we may find the same dull monotony of raiment, architecture, and habits in the Orient as in the Occident.

Photography. Nowadays almost every traveller carries about with him, like some familiar fiend, an instantaneous camera of sorts. But this is by no means welcome in Arab lands; men scowl and mutter " *Ina'la l'Allah ala' elmusawirin* " (the curse of

Allah be on those who take portraits); women bid little girls cover up their faces; small boys grimace, and have been known to run away even from the temptation of proffered pennies. This is due partly to a superstition, partly to a Koranic ordinance. The superstition is that, if you take any one's photograph, you have the power to bring disease and misfortune on him by stabbing his likeness with pin-pricks. The Koranic ordinance forbids the reproduction of the human image in any form,—some say also the image of "anything which casts a shadow,"—as this is to usurp the function of the Creator. Tradition adds that, in the next world, the makers of images will be haunted by their creations, all clamouring to receive souls. "I had no desire to be called into being," an image will say, "but as thou art responsible for my existence, complete thy work and bestow upon me a soul." And, as this is beyond the power of the image-maker, he will be haunted everlastingly. If, however, he be an infidel, and one, therefore, who has no abode in the realms of bliss, the image may have recourse to its living likeness, if a Moslem, and his eternity may be made miserable as an accessory to the sin of an infidel.

The Aïssawas. More than anything else at Kairwān I had anticipated with interest the sight of an orgy of the Aïssawas. I had heard much of the hideous tortures they endure unflinchingly, and of the impressiveness of their barbaric ritual, but I came away with grave doubts as to the genuineness of their performance. They lay themselves out too much for the gratification of tourist curiosity to pass muster as a serious religious body. Instead of scowling on the Rumi intruder, as good Moslems should in a mosque, they hasten to provide him with a front seat, they exhibit all their apparatus for his inspection with the zeal of professional conjurers, and, if he pay well, they will even give extra performances for his sole benefit.

I found a dark pillared room adorned with coloured glass balls, ostrich eggs, and pictures of Jinns. In the centre a number of young men were beating tom-toms furiously and shouting something unintelligible, while every one present kept time with hands and heads in order to induce the hypnotic state. When the hubbub had lasted long enough for this purpose, a number of volunteers stood up in line and swayed to and fro, as the howling Dervishes do in Turkey, keeping time with the drum-beats. Then, one after the other, at intervals, they rushed forward yelling, whirled their heads about, and tore off all their upper garments. Long dull knives were handed to them, and they made a great show of running the blades and points into their flesh. They even employed attendants to hammer the hilts with much noise and apparent vigour. But though the performers had all the appearance of being under the influence of hypnotism, they certainly took good care to do themselves no hurt.

The stabbing was done, much as I have seen it on the stage, with a slight, scarcely perceptible pause just before the incidence of the blow. Moreover, not only was there no blood shed, but never even an indentation of the flesh, as would have been the case with a real blow inflicted in the hypnotic condition. One Aïssawa careered proudly with a thin blade struck through the upper skin of his shoulder; but any one can do this with impunity if he take the precaution of first separating the outer skin. Scorpions were duly swallowed, and it was an horrible sight to see the expression of the hypnotized boys crawling on all fours and staring wistfully at the dispenser of these creatures. But I imagine it would have been easy to remove the stings in advance.

As to the doses of glass, I am less clear. It certainly seemed to me that round pieces were placed in the men's mouths; but there may have been sleight of hand, and the glass may have been removed afterwards. The noise was too incessant for me to hear whether the glass was crunched by the teeth.

The whole scene was chiefly remarkable for the wild agitation—I cannot call it fervour—of the performers. In a state of semi-nudity, with staring eyes and streaming cheeks, they rushed round the mosque, they leaped, they crawled, they shouted in mad rivalry of the deafening drums. It was an hideous pandemonium; yet all seemed entirely under the control of their chief, a grave and reverend Sheikh, who never relapsed for an instant from his imperturbable coolness, and was able at any moment to repress any excess with a look or a touch. I am told that in private life the Aïssawas are, oddly enough, the mildest mannered of men and entirely averse from all thoughts of fanaticism.

Shrines and Seers. One of the most conspicuous landmarks of Tunis is a hill surmounted by a dazzling white dome, whither pious Moslem women are wont to flock in pilgrimage to venerate the sepulchre of an holy lady. Not long ago a *merabut* announced that it had been revealed to him in a vision that the holy lady's sepulchre was in another place. Search was made and as, sure enough, bones were found where the vision had indicated, there seemed no further room for doubt. The pilgrimage was accordingly diverted; the *merabut* built a shrine and began to grow fat upon the offerings of the faithful. But the reward of the seer's inspiration was naturally distasteful to the guardians of the original shrine, who found themselves as wofully neglected as the priests of Diana at Ephesus. Saving the French occupation, they had doubtless set all Tunis in an uproar. As it was, they resorted to more modern methods, an appeal to the Courts resulting in an injunction and damages against their rival, whose vision was not held to be sufficient proof in law. It was, perhaps, the strangest part of the affair that the pilgrims, who had believed in the vision, readily accepted the decision, and returned with devotion unimpaired to their former haunt, which now flourishes more securely than ever.

The Merabut of Baghdad. From a window in Tunis I could see a small mosque dedicated to the memory of a Saint or *Merabut* at Baghdad, and it was a constant delight to observe the passage of his devotees.

There was one old woman in particular who was a regular attendant. She would station herself in front of the great door, which was thickly studded with nails, some of them in the form of lyres and other charms against the evil eye. She would raise her hands in the attitude of prayer, pass them reverently over her face, clutch the heavy iron knocker, and beat a loud tattoo. Then there was a long pause, as if she expected some one to open for her. But no one ever came; for it is understood that the knocker's only use is to engage the attention of the Baghdad Saint. The operation of praying, stroking the face, and knocking was repeated several times, more or less according to the urgency of the case. I have seen her spend half an hour and nearly batter down the door; I have seen her spend five minutes and content herself with the most perfunctory rat-tats. But she has never omitted to conclude the ceremony by solemnly turning over a stone near the door with her stick. On emergencies she has also torn off a shred from her clothing and tied it to the bar of the window. Each procedure was designed to remind the *merabut* of her visit, lest he should be disposed to forget. Some of us tie knots in our handkerchiefs. She preferred to tie a portion of her dress to a window. The principle is the same.

The Story of a Jinn. As an instance of the old-world atmosphere at Tunis and the survival of ideas which were in vogue when the *Arabian Nights* first took literary shape, I may relate a story which was gravely told me by an Arab friend the other day. He was driving into Tunis not very long ago, and had just reached the city gate when his carriage stopped and he found a negro, sixteen feet high, barring the way with a drawn sword. Alighting from his carriage, he asked the negro's will. "You have," was the reply, "an old chest containing papers in your house. I wish you no evil; but if you refuse me that chest, I must kill you and take it." "I will give you the chest," my friend replied; "but if you come to fetch it, you will frighten all my children into fits." "Let not that trouble you," returned the Jinn for a Jinn it was—"place it on your roof to-night. I will fly down and fetch it." My friend did as he was bid, and lo! in the morning the box had disappeared. He is sure that he was in full possession of his senses throughout the interview, and his coachman is equally convinced that he beheld the Jinn.

There are very few Arabs who disbelieve altogether in Jinns. Those who may not believe in good Jinns generally believe in bad ones, and you may hear plenty of stories of people being possessed by them. In that case there is a great ceremony to exorcise the Jinns, incense being burnt, and all the neighbours dancing round the possessed person to the accompaniment of loud drums and every sort of incantation. Nearly all the old mosaics and decorations of doorways in Tunis contain representations of the heads of Jinns or Afreets. An Afreet differs from a Jinn in that he is always evil, and has a horrid contorted countenance.

The great preoccupation, not merely among Mu

hammadans but among Jews and all other aboriginal inhabitants of Tunisia, is to ward off the evil eye. The chief safeguard against this is an outstretched hand, either the so-called hand of Fatima, which is worn in gold and silver and common metals, and painted up over walls and doorways, or as horns and upturned horseshoes, roughly representing the thumb and little finger with the rest of the hand clenched. Oddly enough, while the five fingers are considered a safeguard in this way, the figure five possesses the worst possible reputation. It is the unluckiest of numbers, and any one requiring to use it in bargaining or conversation is expected to use the words "the total of your hand" instead. Otherwise he provokes the retort "*Fi a'inek*—Have it in your eye!"—in other words, may the unlucky number retort upon yourself and blast your eye as a penalty for having ventured to mention it. Other favourite amulets are an axe, a bean set in gold, a coral phallus, and various jingling whirligigs, used more particularly for warding off the evil eye from horses. A snake-charmer generally wears at his waist a brass embossed tablet and a leather pouch with the hand of Fatima upon it. Inside this pouch he often carries a piece of black stone, probably of meteorite origin, picked up at the amphitheatre of El Jem, and supposed to be very potent against the bites of serpents. Other people wear little round leather discs with magical herbs sewn up inside them, or else pouches containing holy names or extracts from the Koran inscribed by magicians upon pieces of parchment. My

Amulets.

teacher of Arabic told me that he was somewhat of a sceptic in matters of religion, but that it was impossible for him to disbelieve altogether in amulets. Some years ago he had been entrusted with one for a short time, and he found, as he had been promised, that while it was in his possession no one could refuse him anything. He had only to wear it in his turban or hold it in his hand, and everything went well; but if he left it at home, or lent it to any one else, nothing succeeded with him.

The hand of Fatima is sometimes called the hand of Ali. She was the daughter of the Prophet, pronounced by him to be one of the three perfect women in the world's history, the other two being the Blessed Virgin and the wife of Muhammad, who proved her faith in him by marrying him when he was only a poor servant. The story goes that another of the Prophet's wives asked him why she had not been included among the perfect women, whereupon he replied that it was for the very good reason that she was by no means perfect. She had married him in the days of his success, whereas the other wife had proved herself the first believer, marrying him and acknowledging him as Prophet when he was poor and of no account.

In the interior of Tunisia there is a greater variety of amulets, many of them derived from the negroes. When I was there, I came across an American traveller, whose hobby it was to collect amulets all over the world for presentation to a New England museum. He was very unpopular among the natives, for the

French authorized him to seize any amulets he might take a fancy to on the doors of the native dwellings; and it was poor compensation for people, who believed that he was taking away with him their only safeguard against misfortune and their best promise of prosperity, to receive a few francs in exchange for these priceless possessions, which had been handed down through countless generations.

Fortune-tellers. It is natural among a superstitious people that recourse should be had to all manner of fortune-tellers; but they surround themselves with almost as much mystery as the more orthodox professors of religion. Accordingly, it is by no means easy to approach them, particularly the more serious and reputable ones. I made many inquiries, however, and pressed my guide to do the like. One day he informed me that he could take me to an old negress, who had a great reputation, and when I told him to insist that the witch should keep any evil prophecies to herself, he replied that there was no need for alarm, as her kind always did so. When I inquired as to her methods, he told me that she would either drop melted lead into water, and prophesy according to the shape which it took; or she would divine with sand or coffee grounds; or she would produce an arrangement of wood, string and charcoal, which, when held by an inquirer answered questions in some way, evidently after the manner of planchette.

We reached the house, which was in a remote and disreputable-looking part of the Arab quarter, and were led up a narrow winding stair by an evil-looking negro, who had acquired a wild animal's skill in going about everywhere with bare feet. When we emerged upon a verandah, overlooking

A FORTUNE TELLER.

the patio of the house, we found a great number of Arab women lounging about without their veils, and they set up a loud protest at the intrusion of men. The negro explained that we were on our way to see the fortune-teller; but this did not pacify them, and there was soon such a hullabaloo in progress that I thought we had better retreat.

Now, however, the witch herself appeared on the scene, quite the most villainous old hag I have ever set eyes on, as black as pitch, as bald as a coot, marked with small-pox until you almost doubted whether she could really be a human being, and possessed of wolfish eyes, which pierced you through and through. She rated the guide furiously for having ventured to come up. There was no objection to *Rumis* (Christians) coming, but that an Arab should intrude where Arab women were sure to be about was intolerable. It would injure her reputation. What kind of an Arab could he be who did not know better than that? I thought she was going to scratch out his eyes; and she was no whit appeased when he faltered meekly that he was a stranger in Tunis, and knew no better. The woman proposed that we should stay and have our fortunes told without him; but our stock of Arabic was so slender that we could have understood very little, so it was arranged that we should come another day, with a Frenchwoman who spoke Arabic, but this, somehow or other, never came off.

Having failed here, the guide sought to redeem his reputation by taking us to a male fortune-teller, a few steps away from the tram-line and the square where the snake-charmers usually perform. Entering a little room on the ground floor, we found a distinguished-looking man seated at a wooden table. He wore a handsome gold turban round his *sheshia*, a gold-embroidered *jebba*, and gold-rimmed spectacles; he had a cast in his eyes, and very ivory teeth.

After the usual elaborate compliments, he made me hold an Arab bamboo pen in my hand, and bade me either wish for something or else ask a question in my mind. When I had done so and returned the pen to him, he put his head on one side, as if waiting for an inspiration, and made a great number of dots, in rows one underneath the other, like an inverted pyramid. Then he proceeded to join certain of the dots with lines, and repeated the operation several times over, obtaining a total from each group of dots and enclosing it in a circle. After further calculations, he began to talk rapidly for some minutes, after which the guide gave me the gist of what he had been saying. On the whole he seemed to have divined fairly well what I had been thinking about, though it would have been impossible to guess it in the ordinary way. He was inclined to ask me a great many questions after his first long speech; and though I did not answer him, he may have gathered something from the expression of my face. When I inquired what I had to pay, he replied that his art was beyond all price, but he accepted with gratitude the small coin which I laid upon his table. With Mrs. Vivian he was less successful, going off upon an entirely wrong tack, and refusing to be set right; but apart from that he contrived to tell her one or two surprising things.

Chapter V

JEWS AND NIGGERS

The Jews of Tunis—"Leghorns"—Industries—Nomad Camp-followers—Education—Rapacity—Anti-Semitic Riots—Organization—Poor-Laws—Law-Giving—The Jewish Quarter—Houses—Religion—Ritual—Saints—Guardian Angels—The Sabbath—Missions to Jews—Food—The Family—A Wedding—A Funeral—Literature and Art—Negroes

The Jews of Tunis. Tunis is one of the chief resorts of Hebrews on the Mediterranean. They are of mixed race and origin, and many of them are difficult to distinguish in appearance from civilized beings. The Syrian element does not predominate, and a large proportion of their ancestors may have been the fair-haired Amorites. Vulture-noses are by no means characteristic.

"Leghorns" The most Hebrew-looking are those who came originally from Leghorn. These have a different ritual, and in 1824 obtained a separate administration from the Bey, which lasted until 1895. They form a kind of Jewish aristocracy, and are now among the most strenuous opponents of the French occupation. In the days when Jews were restricted to a particular costume, they obtained the privilege of wearing a distinctive white cotton cap, but now they have taken to wearing European tweeds and the *sheshia*.

Industries. Unlike most other Jews, those of Tunisia occupy themselves largely with manual labour, their favourite occupations being tailoring, bootmaking, embroidery, weaving, tinkering, and the manufacture of gold and silver ornaments. They have also a great many butchers' shops, which are under the control of the rabbis, who also fix the price of meat and levy a tax upon it for charitable purposes. They seem to have adopted in nearly every case the industries neglected by the Arabs. Originally the Arabs, wearing little more than a blanket, needed no tailors, and the Jews obtained the monopoly of tailoring. A whole street in the bazaars is given up to Jewish tailors, and there is scarcely a house in the whole Jewish quarter which does not contain a tailor's work-shop. Oftener than not, this is little more than a recess, open to the street, where you may observe the tailors, bending over their work with circular backs and plying their needles in feverish haste. It is curious that the Jews should have obtained a practical monopoly of gold and silver work. It was probably found impossible to keep them away from the precious metals, but their designs are always in the worst possible taste.

If the Jews are not artistic, they are at any rate ingenious, and there is no limit to the variety of things for which they will find some practical use. Petroleum being largely used in Tunisia, there is a great accumulation of the tins in which it has been conveyed.

These have become the principal material for the Jewish ironmonger, and traces of them are to be found all over the country. In the interior your water is nearly always brought up in an old petroleum tin, with a wooden bar fitted across the top as a handle, and I have also seen it used for making saucepans, flower-pots, walls, drums, and almost everything except hats.

Nomad Camp-followers. In some parts of the interior there are still groups of Jews living in tents among the nomadic tribes of Arabs, as they have done from time immemorial. They appear to be descended from Berbers who adopted the Jewish religion, and for the most part they earn their living as blacksmiths. Before the French occupation Jews were not allowed to live outside their quarter, but now they are gradually spreading into the French part of the town.

Education. They greedily seize whatever educational advantages the French have to offer, nor do they shrink even from attending missionary schools, and glibly repeating Christian prayers and hymns and creeds which they do not profess to believe for a moment. In another generation or two we shall find in Tunis an educated Jewish population, cherishing no sympathies with the French Government or any form of European civilization, and able to beat any commercial rivals out of the field. Their subtle ingenuity will certainly constitute a greater menace to French colonial enterprise than any possibility of an Arab rising. One difference between the Jew and the Arab is that while an Arab will forget what he has learnt in an European school when he gets home, a Jew is accompanied to school by his women-kind, who are just as eager to learn as himself.

Rapacity. The Jews of the town of Tunis alone are more numerous than those in the whole of Algeria. They are not, however, so thoroughly "distilled," and the race hatred is accordingly far less developed, particularly as the Arabs of Tunisia are much milder than those of Algeria. The Tunisian Jews, however, like most others, are up to all sorts of tricks, among which fraudulent bankruptcies are the favourites.

Their method of bankruptcy is to conceal a large portion of their property, live in ostentatious poverty until their neighbours have begun to forget them, and then start business again with a clean slate. By repeating this process at intervals of a few years they often become very rich. They are also extremely loth to pay the people they employ. I heard a hard case which happened the other day at Gabes. Some Jews obtained a contract to supply the garrison of Mednin, fifty miles away, with corn and hay. They engaged a number of Arabs to effect the transport at a miserably low rate of pay, and then tired them out by an endless succession of subterfuges, until they abandoned all hope of securing even their pittance. It is certainly regrettable that the French authorities, with their theories of paternal government, should not take steps to render such incidents impossible.

In Tunis, just as much as anywhere else, the chief occupation of a Jew is the handling of money. At almost every street corner you may see the tables of the money-changers covered with piles of copper coin, and in every case conducted by Jews. Their religion forbids them to practise usury among themselves, but they evade this by having recourse to a go-between, whose commission naturally increases the interest. He borrows the money from one Jew in order to lend it immediately to another, and in this case the interest generally amounts to ten or twelve per cent. When a Jew lends to an Arab, he naturally exacts a great deal more.

Anti-Semitic Riots. During the riots in Algiers, Tunis plumed herself on her peaceable attitude towards the Jews; but not long afterwards a disturbance took place and, by the negligence of the authorities, was permitted to assume serious proportions. The affair was brought on by the Jews, who lost their heads when one of their number had been wounded in the course of some slight altercation. They barricaded themselves in a house, climbed on to the roof, tore up the parapet of masonry, and proceeded to pelt persons in the street indiscriminately. Then a band of them broke into the mosque attached to a *zawia* or hostelry for poor Muhammadans, and desecrated it in a peculiarly disgusting manner. This provoked demonstrations on the part of the Arabs, which it should not have been difficult to suppress at once. The French authorities, however, displayed so much weakness that business remained at a stand-still, and the native quarters in an uproar, for several days. I mingled with the crowd of Arabs, and found it decidedly good-humoured. The Jewish quarter presented a curious sight when I drove through it one afternoon. Heavy iron shutters had been pulled down over almost every shop front, and an occasional Jew stood peering out of his doorway, ready to dart in and barricade himself at the first alarm. Most of the men, however, had taken refuge in crowds on the flat roofs, and stared sourly at the rare traffic, while the women, dressed in their bright velvets and rabbit-skins, as on their sabbaths and hey-days, thronged the narrow grated windows. Anxiety hung heavy on the air, and it seemed as if the quarter were in instant apprehension of an invading army.

I heard many complaints of the hardships undergone by the poorer Jews, particularly the tailors, who toil early and late for a pittance, and, living from hand to mouth, were destitute after four days' enforced idleness. As, however, the Jews began the trouble, it was impossible to feel surprised that the Arabs should have retaliated, particularly when we remember the state of subjection of the Jews in Tunisia not so very long ago.

Under the Beys, Jews were forbidden to wear light burnuses or fezzes with a tassel, which is considered an emblem of the Moslem faith; they were forced to attach a sleigh-bell to their clothes, that the faithful might be warned of their approach; they might ride asses outside the walls, but nowhere and under no circumstances horses; when they passed a mosque they were compelled to take off their shoes and carry them; and they were always at the beck and call of any Moslem who might require them to fag for him. Often, when the streets were wet, an Arab would hail the nearest Jew to carry him on his back to the opposite pavement. Even under the French regimen it is the custom to address a Jew as " Pig, son of a Pig," " Dog, son of a Dog," " Carrion," " Kaffir," and " Judas," as a matter of course and without special ill-will or provocation.

It therefore speaks much for the sober temper of the Arab population in Tunis that the troubles should have passed off so easily. No lives were taken and few serious wounds inflicted. Indeed, the attitude of the Arabs often recalled to me that of boys engaged in a cat hunt, knowing that the pastime was forbidden, and enjoying it all the more thoroughly for that. A local journal reported that the Arabs congregated in crowds, which maintained an impassive demeanour while the police were about, but, when they fancied themselves unobserved, gave way to a *gaité parfaitement déplacée*!

Organization. The Jews of Tunis form a state within a state, and deserve attention in view of the possibilities of an independent Jewish nation being one day established in Palestine, or at the bottom of the sea. No doubt, the Jews have occupied a position of subjection in Tunisia, but, on the whole, they have probably been better off there than in most other countries. On one occasion, Tunis actually went to war with Venice solely to defend their rights. The Jews are admissible to most public functions, especially in their own particular province of finance. The receiver-general of finance has always been a Jew, and he now also occupies the position of *kaïd* of the Jews. He is nominated, subject to the Bey's approval, by the chief rabbi and the various notables and notaries. He possesses a veto upon the decision of the common council, and, like other *kaïds*, is a judge with power to condemn to fines, imprisonment, and the bastinado.

Poor-Laws. The object of all Hebrew law-giving is not so much to punish as to prevent, and great efforts are accordingly made to do away with all the pretexts of crime founded upon want. There is a tax of 2*d.* a lb. on all meat purchased by Jews, as well as an impost of £4,000 to £8,000 on the Jewish slaughter-houses. In addition to this, there is a sort of voluntary progressive income tax, which is very generally paid. Out of this income, over 6,000 paupers are annually relieved to the extent of some 8*s.* a head, a general distribution of alms is made at Easter, and education is endowed.

Law-Giving. The sentences of the Jewish tribunal are carried out by the Moslem authorities, and they generally err on the side of leniency. Efforts are also made by the Hebrew authorities to check sharp practice and even excessive competition between Jews.

If a Hebrew state ever came into existence, we should probably find that there was no army and scarcely any police, and that most of the judgments depended upon a kind of rough equity, while the regulations of commerce and the safeguards against property had a distinct tinge of socialism.

The chief grievance of the Jews is that, besides being amenable to their own tribunals, they are also subject to those of the Arabs. They complain that, when there is a lawsuit between a Jew and an Arab, the Arab tribunal generally contrives to stretch a good many points in favour of a co-religionist. Very often a Jew will make a fictitious transfer of his claims to a friendly Arab, who sues in his stead and has a better chance of obtaining justice. In criminal cases, too, the Arabs are not tender to the Jews. There was a case, not many years ago, of a Jew being summoned before the Arab tribunal, for blasphemy against Jesus Christ, who was set down in the charge as a great Muhammadan Saint. The man's crime had consisted in the crucifixion of a rat, and he was sentenced to seven weeks' imprisonment.

The Jewish Quarter. When you have passed through the Gate of France at Tunis, you feel that you have crossed the threshold from Europe into Africa. A street on the left takes you to the Arab bazaars, while a street on the right plunges you at once into the thick of the Jewish quarter. Nowhere else, surely, may you see streets so narrow or so dirty. Even the ghettos of Frankfort or East London cannot compare with this. From the opposite windows of the high houses it is an easy step. Every ugly smell, from the penetrating effluvia of fried fish to the sickening odours of rags and rotting meat,

GATE OF FRANCE

confronts you. In every shop and corner are black masses of sluggish flies, and, still more revolting, insects feasting upon a wealth of offal. The streets take all sorts of unreasonable curves as the fancy seizes them, and houses project or retire from the roadway in the most hopeless disorder. On either hand are blind alleys and dark cellars, suggestive of hideous mysteries.

Houses. The Jews are not exclusive as the Arabs are, and there is not the same difficulty about obtaining admission to their houses. You need but to walk through the quarter at any time— a Saturday afternoon for choice if you wish to study the costumes,—ask the children lounging at the door of any house whether you may come in, and they will paw the air at once with a gesture intended to beckon you in. You find a courtyard, as in the Arab houses, and all the rooms open on to it. As a rule, excepting in the case of rich Jews, each room is the home of a separate family, and Jewish families are as large here as elsewhere. How they stow themselves away is a standing puzzle, and you are constantly reminded of a rabbit-warren.

The furniture of a room seems to consist of a table, like the section of a tree-trunk, mounted on stumpy legs, and of a huge family-bed, capable of holding a dozen persons at a pinch. There is a wardrobe, or merely a packing-case, to contain the Sabbath finery, and that is about all. In one corner is a stove with a number of grimy pots and pans. A heavy indefinable odour of drains, dirt, horrible cookery, oppresses the air, and you are very glad to come out again as soon as possible. Directly you make a movement to depart, the whole family, from the venerable patriarch with his long, grimy beard to the half-naked urchin scarcely able to toddle, stretch out their hands with one accord and clamour for money; but if you are wise, you will content yourself with giving a small lump sum, instead of distributing doles to a crowd, which you could never hope to satisfy.

Religion. The difference between a Jewish rabbi and a Christian priest is well illustrated by the fact that, while a priest blesses his congregation in the name of God, a rabbi is content to bless God in the name of the congregation. The rabbi, indeed, possesses very little of the ecclesiastical character. Only if he be a butcher or a circumciser are any special qualifications required of him, and these amount to little more than that he shall be able to tell good meat from bad and to sharpen a knife properly. Similarly, a synagogue has very little to distinguish it from an ordinary house. The rabbi often lives in part of it, and most of the ground floor may be given up to shop-keepers and money-changers. As a rule there is merely a courtyard, where the men assemble, and a gallery for the women. No attempt is made to keep the place tidy, still less to beautify it. The floor is generally paved with ugly tiles, cracked and unwashed, and in one case I noticed upon the walls a series of deplorable lithographs depicting the King of Sardinia, a President of the French Republic, and Frith's Derby Day. A German traveller has compared the synagogues of Tunis to a stock exchange or a coffee-house. Every one lounges about, discusses current events in a loud voice, chaffs and laughs, in a way quite inconsistent with any idea of sanctity attaching to the house of prayer. The sermons are even more irreverently jocular than those of the late Mr. Spurgeon, and it is by no means unusual for one of the congregation to interrupt the preacher in a ribald way, or engage upon an angry discussion with him.

So little does any particular sanctity attach to a synagogue that any private house, where ten persons are gathered together, may be regarded as a synagogue for all practical purposes. A Jew attains his religious majority at the age of thirteen. Then, as was the case with Christ, he is taken to the synagogue to show that he can read the Scriptures and answer an interrogatory upon Hebrew ritual and dogma. After this, he has the right to wear a linen veil over his shoulders on ceremonial occasions, and he is expected to fast and pray regularly.

<small>Ritual.</small> The anti-Semites of Tunis firmly believe that the Jews there kidnap Christian children, to drink their blood during the ceremonies of passover, and this belief has been so generally established in all countries since so many centuries, that it is impossible to reject it altogether, though proofs are by no means easy to obtain, particularly in a country where the registration of deaths is non-existent.

When a Jew is about to pray, he touches his forehead with a copy of the Scriptures and twists a leather strap ten times round his left arm as a symbol of restraining evil thoughts and leaving free current to the good. Unlike the Christian and the Muhammadan, he never uses a rosary.

The Jews, unlike the Arabs, are more strict in the observance of their religion in the country than in the towns. At one place I heard of a Jew who took the trouble to carry a fowl ten miles, in order to have it killed by his rabbi, and, the rabbi being away at the time, brought the bird home again patiently, and went without his dinner. In many towns, however, it is quite common to find the young Jews go to European restaurants for their dinner, and eat the ordinary food, not excepting pork. One would accordingly expect to find them unusually easy-going, but, as a matter of fact, they are a great deal more fanatically anti-Christian and anti-Muhammadan than the old-fashioned Jews, who observe the letter of the law strictly.

Saints. It is probably from the Muhammadans that Tunisian Jews derive their veneration of Saints. Indeed, some of them go so far as to repair to Muhammadan places of pilgrimage, and to burn candles in the *zawia* of Sidi Mahrez, who was the first to permit Jews to dwell inside the city. The favourite Jew saint is a certain rabbi Simon, who happened to be the last man to die during an epidemic, and was accordingly supposed to have stayed it by the sacrifice of his own life.

A day is consecrated to his honour, and the Jews then take their children to his shrine in the evening with candles and flowers. They burn there a curious perfume, made up of jasmin and tallow, and drink a great deal of their favourite liqueur to his memory.

Guardian Angels. One evening, when I was in Southern Tunisia, I was surprised to notice a great concourse of Jews struggling to draw water from a well. Inquiring what it all meant, I was told: "We Jews believe that there are legions of guardian angels, who watch over the earth, air, fire and water respectively. We know from tradition that those whose business it is to protect this well change guard once a year on this day, but we cannot tell the precise moment; our rabbis can only assure us that it is between the hours of three and six in the afternoon. As there would, undoubtedly, be a pestilence in the village if water, which had been drawn at the unguarded instant, were drunk, we do not go near the well for the whole three hours; and, as we need water for our suppers, you may understand this scramble now that six o'clock is past." The Jews here are evidently of the sect of the Sadducees, which "believe in angels and spirits."

The Arabs of the neighbourhood have a kindred belief respecting the sea. Their tradition is that on one night of the year, at the stroke of twelve, the water-Jinns relieve guard, and the sea water becomes momentarily sweet. As it is very lucky to taste it in that condition, the whole population, with all the animals, plunge into the water, and, with the help of a vivid imagination, often try to persuade themselves that the sea has lost its saltness.

The Sabbath. The best day for visiting the Jewish quarter is a Saturday, not merely because the finest clothes are to be seen then, but also because there has been a certain attempt at cleaning up the night before. All wear their brightest colours, the women's pantaloons are freshly washed, and their faces elaborately rouged. They seem to idle away the whole day, lounging at the doorways and at the windows. Sometimes there will be as many as twelve or fourteen faces huddled together at one small window, gaping out upon the street, where there is really nothing to see except crowds of children engaged in noisy games. Once when I was walking through with an Arab guide, he was appealed to by a small boy of his own race, whom the little Jews had been teasing. This made him very furious, and he took up the cudgels at once, brandishing a large stick and apostrophizing the crowd as pigs, dogs, and carrion.

The more prosperous Jewesses wear high sugar-loaf caps, with a silk scarf round them, recalling Mother Shipton or Bacon's "mobled queen." Over their white trousers are short silk coats, of the brightest cherry, mustard, or emerald velvet, generally trimmed with rabbit-skins. The Jewish sabbath is by no means an indulgent holiday, apart from the dispensation from work. Not only is there no feasting, because there can be no cooking, but even smoking is forbidden, not because it would in itself

be covered by this injunction. A lax Jew will, no doubt, refuse to be bound by this ordinance, but he will find public opinion against him.

Missions to Jews. There is an active propaganda in Tunis for the conversion of the Jews. Several thousand pounds are spent annually on this weighty work. The tangible result, during more than one decade, has been the conversion, for value received, of one Jew. He stipulated that he should be conveyed to London and given a silk hat; but, once arrived there, he was no longer a quarry, and the Society had nothing more to say to him. So he sold his silk hat and went to the rich Jews, who decided that the only thing to be done was to pack him back to Tunis, where he remains as a living object-lesson of the futility of missions to the Jews.

And yet futility is, perhaps, an excessive term. The Society provides useful schools, where young Jews may learn languages, arithmetic, and other concomitants of commerce on submitting to instruction in the Christian religion. To this they have not the slightest objection, readily reciting hymns and prayers and even creeds, without professing to believe them. One of the missionaries told me that he did not despair, for, though he had made no converts, he thought he was beginning to succeed in persuading his dairyman to cease from adulterating his milk. He had provided himself with a lactometer, and was now devoting all his proselytizing energies to the propagation of pure milk. The lactometer only showed faint progress, but even that convinced him that Jewish milkmen at least need not wholly be despaired of.

Cardinal Lavigerie's methods generally consisted in appealing to Jews and Arabs by flattery and works of beneficence. His missionaries, the White Fathers of Carthage, are dressed up in a kind of caricature of Arab dress, and his cathedral is rendered even more hideous than it would otherwise have been by the adoption of a parody of Arab architecture. Food and money have been lavishly distributed to native households, and the White Fathers have spared no pains to administer medical relief in more or less amateur fashion. The only result, however, has been that the natives, both Arabs and Jews, have accepted whatever benefits were offered, and, except in a few unsatisfactory cases, have clung steadfastly to their own religions.

Food. The Jews consume almost as much *kuskus* as the Arabs, but it is infinitely nastier, being prepared without the scrupulous cleanliness which the Arabs owe to their religion, and having every kind of offal included among the ingredients. Otherwise there is very little difference in the food, unless it be the inordinate consumption of *bukhra*, a particularly repulsive kind of anisette, in which fermented figs form one of the principal ingredients.

The Family. The chief object among the Jews all over the world is to multiply their race as much as possible. "Those who do not marry," says the code of the rabbis, "are as homicides." To abstain from having children is considered as bad as taking away life, and all the regulations of the Jewish family have their first concern with this. Polygamy is permitted, but in Tunis it is rarely practised unless the first wife has no children, and even then it is often found simpler to divorce her and take some one else in her place. Marriages with Gentiles are forbidden, not so much on account of the exclusiveness of the race, as on account of a theory that such marriages only produce daughters. Until recently a childless widow was obliged to marry her brother-in-law, and, if he refused, she had the right to have him before the Courts and go through a ceremony of tearing off his shoes and spitting upon them. To avoid the necessity of this marriage, however, a man will now often divorce his wife when he is on his death-bed.

The drawback to large families in most countries is the difficulty of maintaining them, but the Jews bring up their children to maintain themselves at the earliest possible age. When a boy is thirteen, he is considered responsible for his own actions, and has no claim to be supported by his family. He may acquire real property, make his will, and set up in business on his own account; but should he attempt to alienate his property foolishly, he finds that the law has protected him by tying it up strictly. It is by no means unusual in Tunis to see a young man of eighteen at the head of a large business, which he contrives to direct with considerable skill.

Next to, or perhaps even before, the production of children, the object of a Jewish marriage is the increase of riches. By strict law, a Jewish bridegroom in Tunis must give his bride a dowry of £8, as a protection in case of his dying or divorcing her. In practice he gives a great deal more, as a rule the half of the dowry which she brings with her and which she cannot leave to any one but him. A husband must provide his wife with necessaries, while she must engage herself on some productive labour, however rich she may be. She must wait upon her husband at meals, and take her own afterwards apart, and no one else may make his bed.

A Wedding. One of the chief sights to which the guides are always anxious to conduct tourists, is that of a Jewish wedding. It is the chief event in the history of every Hebrew family, and, in the case of people in easy circumstances, generally lasts three weeks. A fortnight before the ceremony, the bridegroom sends a parcel of embroidered slippers and various garments and cosmetics for the bride's use. Both then proceed in state, accompanied by all their intimate friends, to their separate baths. The bride soaks her hair in a thick, evil-smelling oil, and rubs her body with a paste to remove all the smallest hairs. Then she makes up her eyes and brows with thick layers of kohl, and stains her fingers and toes a ruddy nicotine colour with henna.

Then the bridegroom and his friends come to the bride's house for a game of hide-and-seek. She has cooked a fowl and hidden it somewhere, and the superstition is that whoever finds it will be married within the twelve months. The process of searching causes the utmost merriment, and a great deal of coarse horse-play is indulged in. The actual ceremony does not take place in the synagogue, but in the house of the bridegroom. The staircase has been newly whitewashed, and a large hand has been painted upon it with bullock's blood to ward off the evil eye. The bride's friends have all taken part in dressing her up in all the finery imaginable, silk and tinsel predominating, and she has been decked out with a tremendous weight of silver ornaments and glittering rosettes, which recall a prize ox, particularly in view of her extravagant stoutness, which is considered the chief point of female beauty among the Jews of Tunis. It is only in Tunis and among the negroes of Central Africa that a woman's attractiveness is measured by weight.

I was surprised to find that the men were admitted to the ceremony of dressing the bride. She did not seem in any way abashed, but throughout the whole proceedings she had, according to custom, to remain absolutely speechless. In the courtyard of the house was a little table, beside which the bridegroom awaited her standing. A kind of throne, covered with cloth of gold, hired for the occasion, had been placed there for her, and she took her seat upon it with the grace and manners of a mummy. It was then the bridegroom's business to take great precautions against the possibility of trickery; for a Jew will often substitute a less desirable sister for the intended bride, or else she may have some lover who will seize the opportunity of placing upon her finger his own ring instead of that of the bridegroom, for whom this would be considered an indelible disgrace. When the ring has been duly placed on the bride's finger by the bridegroom, an infernal din is struck up with drums and a kind of crooning song. The bride and bridegroom are solemnly covered over with a large veil, as a token of their union. A glass of wine is brought in, that the bridegroom's various relations and the rabbis may take a sip in turn. There is a frightful scramble among the other guests as to who shall have the good fortune to finish the contents; and, when the glass has been solemnly dashed upon the ground, another scramble for the pieces as mementoes. All this takes place in the bride's house, but next day the festivities are continued with a banquet at the bridegroom's. The bride has been brought to the house, with a great show of reluctance on her part, to the accompaniment of an improvised song setting forth all her merits. The banquet consists almost entirely of pastry and evil-smelling liqueurs. In the centre of the table is a thick yellow wax candle, guttering horribly. The bride sits cross-legged on a pile of cushions at the head of the table, and remains as motionless as ever. She wears many additional scarves of silk and silver, and a number of necklaces of coins, coral, and various amulets.

To my amazement, when I came in, the bridegroom rose, and, before I knew what he would be at, had given me an embrace. I am afraid I was unable altogether to hide my disgust, but I soon soothed all possible susceptibilities by handing over the small present I had brought with me. There was scarce any conversation, and every one seemed entirely satisfied with the occupation of consuming an endless succession of cakes in stolid silence. Conversation would indeed have been difficult in presence of the deafening music, which only ceased to give way to other entertainers,—a conjuror, a juggler, and a man who imitated, without much success, the noises of the various animals known in North Africa. Later on, singing and dancing women were introduced, and the revelry went on far into the night, to be begun again on the following afternoon.

A Funeral. The work of an undertaker among the Jews is not professional but hereditary. It is vested in a body of men known as the "Friends of God," who are especially respected in this world and expect particular privileges in the next. It is their business to lay out a corpse for burial, and, gathering round it, to sing through their noses for a long period, while the women of the family, led by a professional weeper, lament with loud, artificial wails in a neighbouring room. They then carry the body to a tomb, and watch over it for the next three nights.

Literature and Art. In our sense of the words, literature and art are practically non-existent among the Jews. The nearest approach to art is, perhaps, the rude music, which the Jews consider a profession, and have established under the authority of an *amin*, like other trades. No doubt the musicians earn a good deal of money by attending weddings and other revels, but their music is both discordant and monotonous; and I am inclined to think that Tunisian Jews must possess a different ear to other people, or else that the peculiar unpleasantness of their music must have been handed down through a succession of discordant generations.

The same preference for discord is observable in the Jewish costumes, which in theory are very much the same as those of the Arabs.

Negroes. In many respects the negro population is the most agreeable in Tunis. Every face seems wreathed in chronic smiles, and nothing ever seems to disturb their boundless equanimity. It is not so very long since the negroes were all of them slaves, and their emancipation has not yet had any of the evil effects which may be observed in America. The Muhammadan religion had already conferred upon them a certain semblance of equality with their masters, and they have not become bumptious or aggressive. Three or four different complexions and natural characteristics may be noted, apart from the various mixtures due to the infusion of Arab blood. The blackest are those imported from the Sudan, and they may also be distinguished from those born in Tunisia by the fact of their being tattooed. On the faces of some of them may be noticed one or more thin scars, done with a razor each time they were bought or sold. They do not wear a distinctive costume, but the women generally affect a woollen petticoat with red and white stripes. Under no circumstances will they ever wear black, which they hold in particular horror. They even go so far as to avoid any profession which would bring them into contact with black. Their chief ambition is to be employed to whitewash houses, which they do by throwing the whitewash, instead of applying it with a brush.

Chapter VI

IN AND OUT OF TUNIS

Arrival—First Impressions—Streets—Shops—A Street Story-teller—Snake-charmers—The French Quarter—Accommodation—Food—An Anglican Church—Beggars—Marsa—Carthage.

M. ZOLA once told me that, when collecting material for a book, he relies only on the first fortnight's impressions. The more I travel, the more is the wisdom of this reflection brought home to me. After the first fortnight nothing surprises, not even surprising Africa, and fresh wonders only serve to add colour or detail, and at the same time confusion, to the picture begotten by the mind. Accordingly I hastened to set down the prominent features of Tunis while they still remained red-hot in my memory.

Arrival. My steamer's last forty minutes were passed in a narrow brackish canal, flanked by stone moles. The sky was of a thick leaden hue, and, ahead of us, seemed to have come down and enveloped Tunis in a great gloomy burnus. Wide-sailed feluccas, moored by the water's edge, like monstrous dragon-flies, shook their wings impatiently as the waves of the paddle overtook them. On their decks I caught my first glimpses of native

Africans — white teeth grinning a welcome from frameworks of hooded ebony. Above the bows, long files of startled flamingoes sped away to their homes in the fœtid lakes.

The landing-stage at last! The skies had indeed come down. It never rains at Tunis, they say, but it does pour. There had not been so much as a shower for four years and a half, I was told, and nature was evidently making up for lost time.

The scrimmage on the arrival at an Eastern port has already been described too often, but cannot altogether be omitted. A dark, bare-legged gentleman, clad in little more than the old sack which draped his head, had come on board with the post-office tug. He took possession of my twelve trunks, lit a cigarette, and received with a complacent smile the small army of porters who had fought their passage across the regular gangway. Shouldering rather more trunks than he could conveniently manage, and still puffing away at his home-made cigarette, he set out triumphantly for shore. But his triumph was of short duration. The others were not going to submit tamely to seeing all the luggage carried off piecemeal by one man. Each seized upon the nearest trunk and joined the procession. The original porter was furious, and started a vehement altercation, besides which the debates of the Reichsrath were an *agapé*. What wealth of gesticulation, what declamation, what irony, what invective! It was hopeless to intervene, so I struggled through the rain to the Customs-shed, satisfied the Bey's officials that I had nothing to declare, and fought my way to the hotel omnibus. Then the fun began in real earnest. Everybody wanted to be paid. They had had a race from the boat with my luggage, and now expected me to say, like Alice's Dodo, "Everybody has won, and everybody must have prizes." I referred them to the hotel porter, and for a moment he was like to be torn to pieces. Never have I seen so great excitement produced by so slight a cause. The porter was evidently accustomed to such manifestations, and did not share my delight in the dramatic scene. He promptly decided to pay nobody, and bade all claimants run after the omnibus to the hotel. Time is not money in Tunis, so they readily fell in with the arrangement, splashing steadily through the mud and continuing their altercation at the top of their voices all the way.

First Impressions. Next day (December 29th, 1897) the sun reappeared, and I took the first opportunity of driving through the native quarters. The afternoon was like a balmy English May-day, and the deep blue sky formed an exquisite background to the dazzling whiteness of the roofs, domes, and walls. What most impressed me was the dignity and courtesy of the natives. The long white mantle, hanging from their crowns, seemed to add a full cubit to their stature. They stalked, proudly erect, looking neither to the right hand nor to the left, and heeding a collision with a mule or a water-carrier as little as the impudence of little French boys who jeered or tugged at their robes. Whether they were in the poorest of rags or the most brilliant of embroidered cloaks made no manner of difference to their majestic gait. The only puzzle was

TUNIS: A STREET.

how they contrived to hold their heads so high and
strut about so grandly in slippers which did not reach

their heels. You might see a man sitting sideways on the tail end of a little donkey: the man dangled his legs like pendulums, and the donkey jolted unceasingly, but the shoes, poised upon the tips of the toes, remained on as securely as if they were glued.

Streets. Every street was very narrow and the passage of a landau and pair necessarily caused some confusion. But the people never seemed vexed, even when a horse's nose dug them in the back and they had to spring aside and flatten themselves suddenly against the wall. The fatalism of Islam was very apparent in the street scenes. None seemed to take the faintest notice of traffic until the last possible moment, and even when a carriage or tramcar almost ran down an Arab, he stepped aside with the sublimest unconcern.

From your carriage you might observe every variety of raggedness, and it was safe to say that the ragged people were the most dignified. There were men in blankets, in sheepskins, in striped rugs, and in rotten sacking. Their only costume seemed to consist of a voluminous head-dress, intended to reach to the knees. At all costs heads must be covered, but it was quite unimportant how much of the legs might be exposed. This was most striking in the case of the women. Traditional modesty compelled them to cover their faces. Some wore two black veils, leaving the tiniest aperture for their eyes. Others went about like veiled prophetesses of Khorassan, holding the ends of a great curtain which concealed the features. But in the most modest cases the legs were

AB-SUKA SQUARE, TUNIS.

left more bare than would be tolerated in the least squeamish Paris music-hall. The colours of the men's cloaks were entrancing. The softest salmon pink, green, or cornflower blues were to be seen at every corner, and put to shame the most ambitious creations of Paris milliners.

Shops. As everywhere else in the East, the shops were great doorless cupboards open to the street. Except in the bazaars all the goods were spread out to the public gaze, and the vendors reclined on mats, or squatted cross-legged on divans. Never had I seen anything to compare with the natural æstheticism of their arrangement or the brilliancy of their colours. Most charming of all were the fruit-shops, with rows of light blood-oranges festooned upon the rafters, clusters of chillies, like prodigious fairy-lamps illumining the darker corners, and great sacks of glistening dates upon the counters. Even the butchers' shops were picturesque, and it was always a fascination to watch the cross-legged Arabs plying their esparto-switches to keep off the flies, who forgathered even in mid-winter. The hemp and rope shops presented a fascinating array, as did the ironmongeries with rusty chains and huge keys in clumsy locks all dangling at the doors. Driving along, there were charming peeps into native coffee-houses, where rows of turbaned dignitaries lay wrapped in contemplation or played unruffled games of cards. Even in December it was an open-air existence, and the divans outside the shops were studded with contented dreamers.

At every street corner were water-taps, testifying

to the Moslem's teetotalism. All day a succession of water-drinkers might be seen there, many of them armed with strange old-world skins, formed with the whole body of a goat.

<small>A Street Story-teller.</small> Among the most amusing sights was a street story-teller. First he collected his audience in a circle round him by much banging of his tambourine. Then he proceeded to spin the most marvellous yarns, only stopping to collect pennies when he reached a climax of excitement, and perceived that his hearers were burning to know what happened next to the princess, or the Jinn, or the enchanted casket. He reminded me of the sensational magazines, which always take care to close the instalments of their serials at the most breathless situations. When he had collected as much as he fancied would be volunteered by his hearers, he would count up the total and announce that he must have so many more pence before revealing another syllable of the story. He was generally as good as his word, and it was the most inquisitive part of the audience which had to pay. According to the interest of a story and the greed of the teller, the frequency of these demands varied, but they were always introduced with so much humour and ingenuity that no one could possibly resent them.

<small>Snake-charmers.</small> Similar methods are adopted by the snake-charmers. They beat a drum to attract the crowd, and then deposit in the centre of a circle a long pear-shaped basket and a kind of bundle or bag made of old rags. These contain the serpents, which are induced to put their heads

TUNIS: A DOOR.

HINDU SNAKE-HARMER.

out in order to arouse the public curiosity, but the performance itself never begins until a satisfactory collection has been made. The serpent will then follow the charmer round and round the circle while he pipes to it upon a rustic flute, or it will sit up and make furious darts at him when he has subjected it to a long process of teasing. An Arab told me that the fangs of these serpents are never removed, and that most of the charmers come to grief very early in their careers. I believe that what they rely upon is teasing the serpent, and making it dart against its basket or some other hard substance till it has spent its venom; but, even so, it is not appetizing to see the man hold up a serpent in front of his mouth, and allow it to sting his outstretched tongue again and again.

<small>The French Quarter.</small> Though the French do little to attract colonists, I must not omit to record that they lay themselves out to provide what they consider the most important attraction of all. When a Frenchman leaves his native country, he is concerned with solid creature comforts very little, and with scenery, picturesque customs, intellectual interests not at all. But he considers it absolutely necessary at all costs to have what he calls "distractions." If they are absent, he does not consider a place worth living in. Accordingly, serious efforts have been made to render Tunis at least habitable in this respect. There is a modest theatre, where immodest pieces and light opera percolate from Paris, and, despite all their shortcomings, attract crowded houses every night. There is a number of music-halls of the lowest type: a military

band plays from time to time on the main boulevard; a deserted park is being slowly planted with shrubs; and persistent efforts are being made to mould the

STREET CHEESE-SELLER.

wonderful old-world town upon the ordinary commonplace European pattern.

It is true that so far the French quarter has very properly kept itself aloof from the old native town, but encroachments have already begun, and every

PARIS. AVENUE DE L'EAU.

day they become more obtrusive. Lumbering tramways traverse the native quarters in almost every direction, filling up the narrow streets and hustling the stately Arabs against the walls. Many a lovely Arab mansion has had to come down to make room for unnecessary boulevards, which before long will doubtless intersect all Tunis.

Even in the French quarter, however, there are many sprightly scenes : stately camels strutting along superciliously, with their noses high in air; diminutive donkeys, not much larger than a fine S. Bernard dog, laden with baskets of brilliant fruit and accompanied by distinguished Orientals, who emit the most musical of street-cries; mules ridden without bit or bridle by youths in *sheshias*, who sit right back almost upon the animal's tail and guide him by flicking a wand over his ears. Sometimes I have seen two gaunt wheat-sacks walking along hand-in-hand, and, even when I have come up to them, I have scarcely realized that they could contain human beings. At other times I have seen a huge wardrobe lounging down the street, apparently provided by nature with a pair of legs.

Throughout Tunisia both animals and men are used to carrying the most prodigious weights. I have seen a man carry seven chairs, a Chesterfield sofa, a big table, and two small sideboards, all neatly dovetailed together, on his shoulders. A minute donkey will sometimes be laden with three great panniers of oranges, which one would think a heavy load for a horse, and have to carry, moreover, a big, fat Arab, who somehow manages to find room to sit between the panniers and the donkey's tail. Near Bizerta I descried what appeared to be Birnam Wood coming to Dunsinane, but was in reality an Arab horse struggling along under a load of olive-branches. I have hitherto imagined that bearing olive-branches was the exclusive prerogative of doves; but surely the dove-cotes of all Africa could hardly furnish carriers for such a load. The poor horse entirely disappears under it. One occasionally catches sight of a head, and that is all.

The streets of the whole town are infamously paved, and, excepting one or two main thoroughfares, scarcely lighted at all. And Tunis, it must be remembered, is the show place of the Regency. Very few travellers go any further, and if they did so they would certainly fare a great deal worse.

Accommodation. The Grand Hotel and Hotel de Paris, which used to be under the same administration, are those most likely to appeal to European travellers. The Grand is the better furnished and more pretentious, but looks to make a great profit during the short season, and is decidedly extortionate in view of prices at Tunis. Moreover, most important of all, courtesy is lacking, and everything is offered or rather yielded upon the "take it or leave it" principle. The Hotel de Paris would require a large expenditure on furniture and decoration before it could be pronounced altogether satisfactory; but the landlord is the most obliging I have met anywhere, and the cookery is very fair, although the Marseilles fashion of deluging everything with onion and garlic may alarm many. As, however, I spent several

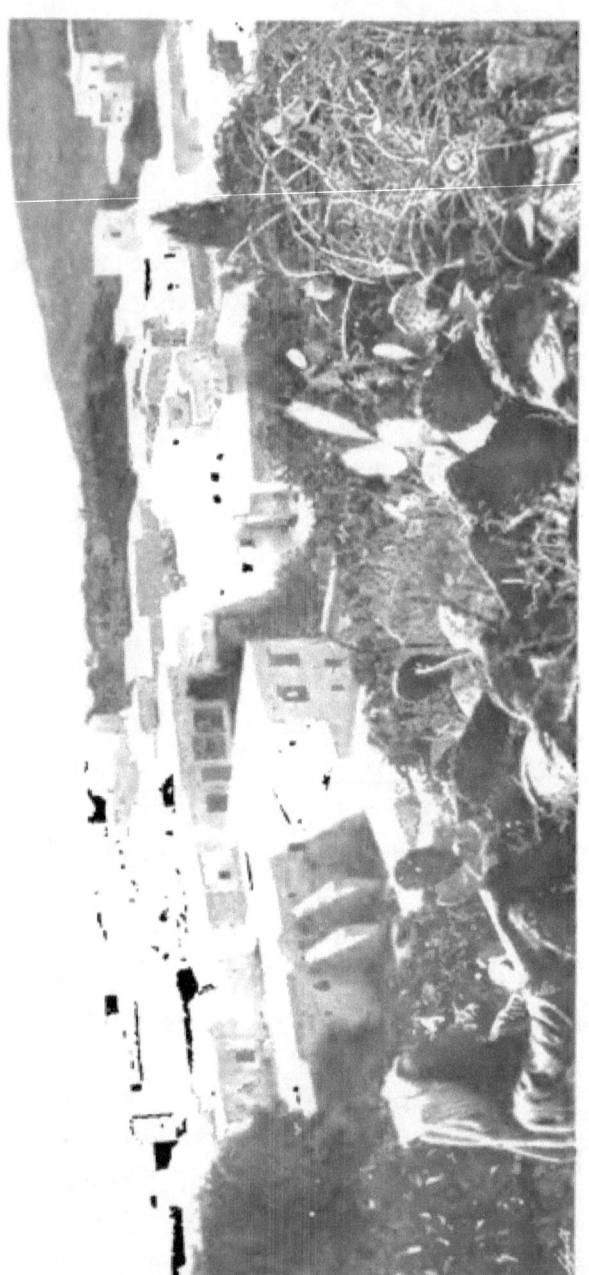

months there and never had occasion for serious complaint, I feel that I can cordially recommend it. Of the second class inns, the Hotel Eymon, otherwise Gigino, is well spoken of, but I was not taken by the appearance or the food when I lunched there.

Food. Good food is extremely difficult to obtain in Tunis. The meat is tough and tasteless beyond description, even when by special effort it has been imported from Marseilles; and the traveller must rely upon the game, which is good but not varied, and the fruit and vegetables, which are excellent. Green peas, new potatoes, and an agreeable wild asparagus, which sells at two large bunches for three half-pence, are a decided attraction at Christmas; and the dates and blood oranges are as good as may be found anywhere. For a long stay, I should advise travellers to bring their own servants, and take an Arab house and an Arab man for the rough work. A staff of Arab servants would be a constant trial even to people intimate with the Arab language and customs. French colonial servants or lodgings are of course quite out of the question, and Italians, Maltese, or Levantines have serious drawbacks.

An Anglican Church. Steps are being taken in Tunis to build an Anglican church. Some years ago a piece of land and an iron church were provided by private munificence. The church was pulled down at a cost of 200 francs and sold for 260 francs—a bad bargain; but the land went up immensely in value, and fetched some £3,000. It is now hoped that the Government may give a site near the British cemetery, and designs are being considered for the erection of a stone church. The next step will be to create a congregation, as at present there is only one resident English family in addition to the Consular officials; but tourists are numerous during the short season, and the erection of an Anglican church may go far to attract others. If the scheme comes to anything, it is to be hoped that proper services may be insisted upon. In the winter of 1897-8 a German missionary officiated in broken English at the Consulate, but his travesty of the Anglican ritual was so offensive that I could not endure it for many minutes. Should there be an appeal for funds for an Anglican church at Tunis, subscribers will do well to make sure in advance that their money will not be diverted to the support of a Protestant conventicle.

Beggars. There are always a certain number of more or less unclothed Beduin women, mostly of the Swassi tribe, running about the streets of Tunis and imploring for alms. "By the head of thy wife," they exclaim to an obviously newly-married man, "give me sous. By the head of *madama*, give, I say. By thy head, give . . . ." They never seem to tire of their chorus, but will run for miles by the side of a carriage or dance before a traveller, carefully impeding his way as he walks through the narrow streets of the Arab quarter. They pluck at his clothes, like greedy hens attacking a feed of corn, and spread their glistening teeth in front of his face, or display a bundle of mouldy babies under his nose. But they are always boundlessly good-natured, and keep their patience though they be tantalized by the hour. From

CARTHAGE: REMAINS OF THE BASILICA.

a bird of passage they will never take "No" for an answer, but when they come to know you and to understand that you are generally good for a few coppers, they may be relied upon for the finest manners in the world. You have but to appeal to them as old friends, telling them that you are not in a generous mood to-day, but to-morrow you will see what you can do, and they instantly scamper off in search of another victim. I was never tempted to give to beggars until I came to Tunis, but there was no resisting the eloquence of these appeals, and it soon became quite an expensive undertaking to walk the length of the street. If, however, I encountered any of my most particular satellites, they would always act as a bodyguard and keep their rivals at a distance.

Only once was I seriously annoyed by beggars. I had bought some pieces of pottery from children at Carthage, and when the bargain was concluded they danced around me demanding other coppers as a present. Finding me obdurate, they trod on my heels and stood in my way, inviting me to hit them with my stick if I dared. Pushes and threats were of no use whatever, and they pointed to some evil-looking huts, from which they said their relatives would come out and defend them. It was looking as if there would soon be a serious row, when we encountered a stalwart Arab coming along the path. I was curious to see whether he would prove a friend or a foe, or whether he would pass by on the other side. To my surprise and delight, he came to my rescue at once, without being asked; and I could hear him upbraiding the children for their shamelessness with great vehemence until I passed out of hearing.

Marsa. The Bey having established his court, such as it is, at the village of Marsa, some twelve miles out of Tunis, the well-to-do families of the town and the various diplomatic representatives have settled there, at any rate during the hot weather. It is connected with Tunis by a rickety light railway, originally belonging to an English company, but until quite lately in the hands of the Italians, who have now been eliciting many protests in their own country by selling it to the French. No doubt if Tunis ever becomes a prosperous and popular resort, Marsa will develop into a kind of superior suburb. At present it affords a pleasant excursion, which may be combined with a visit to Carthage and a picnic at Sidi-bu-said (our Lord the Father of Happiness), a delightfully picturesque little white village on the top of a hill, supposed, according to one tradition, to be dedicated to S. Louis, in remembrance of his having turned Mussulman just before his death. I know few more pleasing views than that from this hill, and no one who visits Tunis should allow himself to be persuaded not to go thither on the first fine day.

Carthage. Apart even from sympathies with the enemies of Rome, a visit to Carthage is laden with melancholy. Modern Carthage consists of little more than a rude mound, surrounded by Cardinal Lavigerie's garish, white-washed cathedral, recalling a glorified Brixton villa, a few pothouses, overlooking a splendid view, and the museum, where some

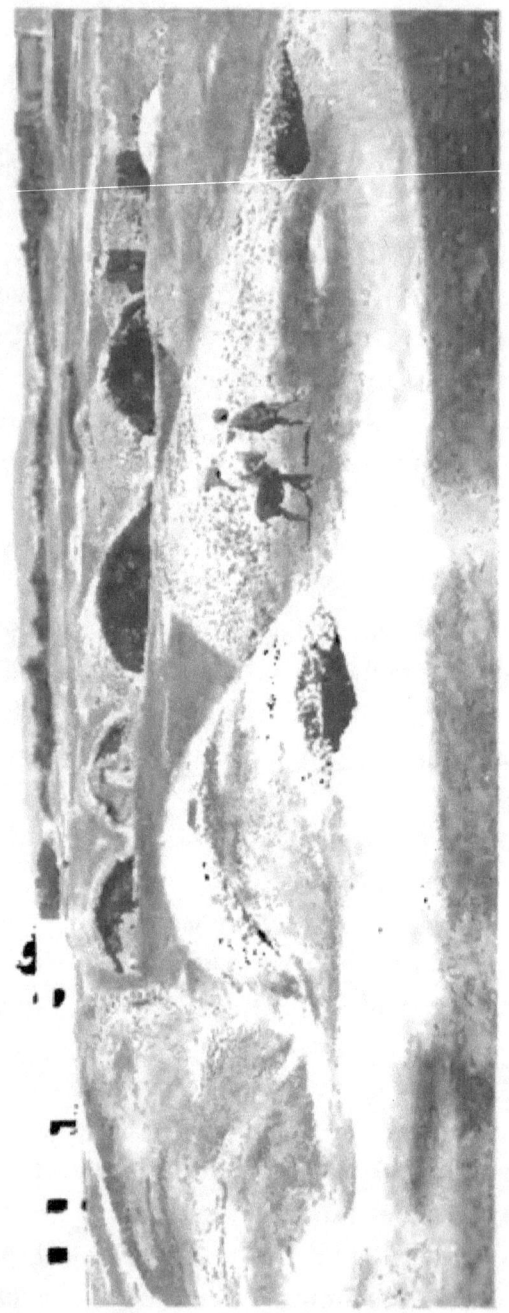

CARTHAGE: OLD CISTERNS OF LA MALGA.

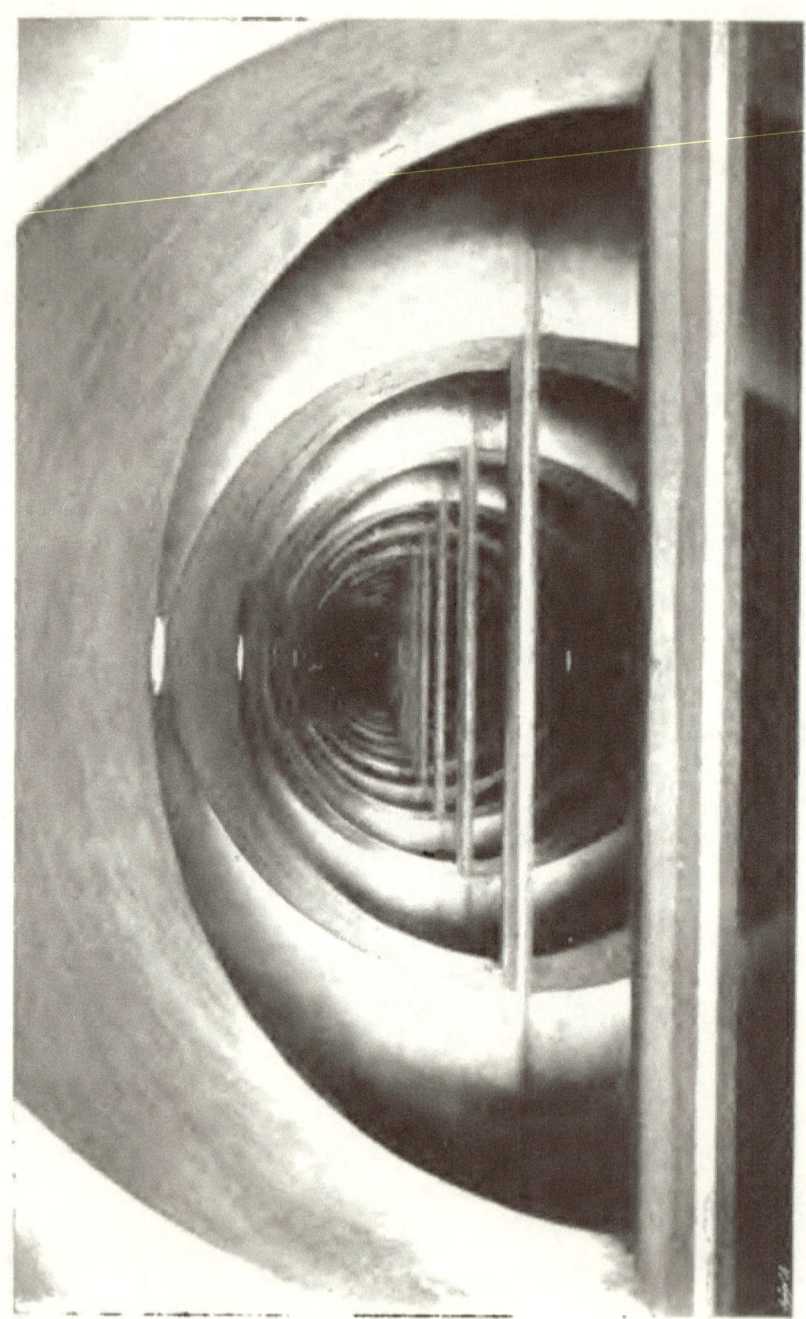

CARTHAGE: RESTORED CISTERNS.

trumpery finds are on view. Practically the whole of Carthage is still underground. Cardinal Lavigerie bought up the land which covers it, with the contents of his missionary boxes; but he and his successors, while rigorously warning off other investigators, have themselves done little more than scrape the ground. A small band of monks, clad in a ridiculous combination of fezzes and white flannel, may be seen shovel-

MONKS EXCAVATING AT CARTHAGE.
(*Photograph by Mrs. Vizetelly*.)

ling earth about in a perfunctory way. If only the French authorities had taken over the work at the beginning of the occupation, the whole of Carthage, with all her archæological and historical riches, might have been revealed long ago.

Serious excavation would doubtless reveal much of historical, but nothing of artistic value, as Carthaginian art was essentially rude and barbarous, while that of the Romans there possessed the rococo character which we associate with Louis XV. The most interesting things in the museum are those which have been found in tombs. It was originally the custom among barbarians to bury with a man all the things he was considered likely to require in the next world—lamps to light him on his path, plenty of money, and enormous provisions of food, generally the legs of antelopes, and whatever else had been among his favourite delicacies,—so that he might find every creature comfort at the moment of his resurrection. Above all, it was necessary to bury his war-horse and his wife with him, that he might not lack those necessaries. Later on, particularly when Christianity had spread its influence, it became usual to bury, instead of a wife, a small Tanagra figure as an emblem.

The museum contains one or two large statues in good preservation but of small artistic value, a certain number of seals, masks, tear-bottles, grotesque figures, and a variety of coins, Vandal, Punic, Roman, Byzantine, etc. The collection of Christian lamps is probably the best in the world, and many of the others are of interest. Ashtaroth, the Phœnician goddess, is in great evidence both on coins and lamps. The favourite Roman emblem seems to have been a Lybian lion with a palm tree growing out of his back. The chief Christian emblems are the fish, the stag, and the lamb, the stag being often represented drinking out of a chalice. Various charms and talismans have also been unearthed, and the following Punic inscription, found

A PUNIC TOMB.

on a crumbling parchment inside a tomb, is not without interest: "I adjure thee, thou spirit of a man who died prematurely, whoever thou mayest be, by the powerful names of Codbaal, Bathbaal, Authogerotabaal, and Basythotisa, that thou keep fast in this vase the images and the horses whose names I now give thee."

In some of the tombs long conduits have been discovered, by which tears and other offerings, poured in at the surface of the soil, might be expected to reach the body of the deceased. These it has been found impossible to preserve, but I have seen photographs of them taken at the moment of excavation.

The configuration of the soil has probably altered a great deal since Carthaginian times, and authorities are by no means agreed as to the position of the various sites. The famous cisterns have been restored so many times that it is now practically impossible to trace any Carthaginian workmanship about them. The ports of Carthage were evidently much larger than they are now, for the land has been constantly encroaching upon the sea. In process of time it will probably fill up the whole of the fœtid lake. It would therefore be futile to attempt to excavate underneath this lake, which has been there from time immemorial and can only contain the various things which may have been dropped into it.

It is unfortunate that the French should consider that the erection of a hideous cathedral absolves them from the necessity of keeping up the chapel of S. Louis. It is no doubt too much to expect modern

Frenchmen to care much for S. Louis, but it would be better to remove the chapel altogether than to leave it in its present indecent condition, with walls peeling off and grass growing among the pavestones.

No visitor to modern Carthage goes there expecting to see very much, but there is a melancholy interest in wandering among the ruins and carrying off pieces of mosaic or Carthaginian bones, and contemplating the completeness of the destruction of the ill-fated city.

As if the work of the Romans had not been sufficiently thorough, it would seem that every one of their successors had set himself to continue the destruction of Carthage. It has become, as time went on, a quarry for the whole world, and even the uttermost of its foundations have been dispersed. The native quarters of Tunis have for the most part been constructed out of the ruins of Carthage, the cathedral of Pisa and many of the palaces and churches of Genoa were made with Punic marbles. A few of the commoner lamps and cameos and other antiquities may be bought from the monk who keeps the door of the museum, but his prices are so extravagant and his collection is so poor that he offers no very serious temptation. From time to time an object of interest may be purchased for a few pence from the Beduin children of the neighbourhood, but they are now so carefully watched by the authorities that anything of value is rarely found in their hands.

And yet Carthage may not altogether be despised, for she is alive with memories. We may pluck corn-

BASILICA AT CARTHAGE.

flowers, whose progenitors were trodden by Dido or Hannibal; we may dream away an afternoon upon the rocks, where the lidless eyes of Regulus were exposed to the fierce rays of an African sun; we stumble over a stone—perhaps it shelters the last sleeping-place of the Vandal Thrasamund. The moral of Carthage, the memory which lingers longest with us, is afforded by the layer of grim ashes which we discover everywhere a few inches below the surface. What a monument to the barbarism of Rome; what a sermon upon the vanity of human glory. Surely none may be so callous as to refuse the tribute of a sigh.

Chapter VII

THE INSIDE OF THE CUP AND THE PLATTER

The Interior—Accommodation—Fonduks—Vermin—Fantasias—Art—Bicycles—An Itinerary—Tunis to Susa—Susa—Susa to Kairwân—Kairwân—Sabra—Susa to Sfax—El Jem—Sfax—Fortifications—Gabes—A Sandstorm—Wells—Jerba—Sbeitla—Thala—El Kef—Beja—The Mejerda—Dugga—Bizerta.

The Interior. THE more I have travelled about Tunisia the more impatient I have grown at the presence of the French. It is not mere patriotism which makes me say that an English occupation would have been a very different matter. No doubt we could not have avoided rubbing off much of the bloom of the Orient, but we should at least have set up the full polish of civilization in its place. The French have not done this, and it is only when we contrive to escape entirely from their contamination that we realize what a paradise they have spoiled. The East is the happy hunting ground of the colourist and ministers to the lust of the eyes more than to any other sense. The silvery whiteness of the houses, the exquisitely soft tints of the men's raiment, the harmonies of the native handicrafts, and the brilliancy of the contrasts at every street corner are a constant delight. It is an inexpressible relief, after being hustled in European towns, to mix with men whose every instinct is courteous and whose calm dignity it seems impossible to ruffle.

<small>Accommodation.</small> The inns in the country districts, where there are any, are exceedingly primitive. They are usually kept by some Levantine who has no notions of cookery or comfort, or by some French colonist who inflates his bill with the least possible expenditure of money and politeness. Perhaps the inn which was at once the most pretentious and the most impossible in the interior, was the Hôtel Splendide at Kairwân. After enduring it for as many hours as I could, I removed to the Grand Hôtel, which proved simple but well managed, and certainly offered far better accommodation than any other I found in my travels after leaving Tunis. At Susa the Hôtel de France was primitive but tolerable. At Sfax there was merely a choice of pothouses, but little cause for complaint if no great expectations were entertained.

At Gabes I was made very welcome and treated very kindly in the Hôtel des Voyageurs, which is kept by a very amiable French woman, who possesses the rudiments of meridional cookery and three or four make-shift bedrooms opening out upon an Arab courtyard. The entrance is through a dingy little shop, which serves as the restaurant, and contains an assortment of venerable groceries and hair washes for the temptation of the colony. There is a more pretentious hostelry over the way, but those who ventured there told me that they had good reason for repentance. There is also an inn at Gafsa on much the same lines; but travellers who persevere further into the interior must trust to the grudging hospitality of the French authorities, or be glad to find a shelter within four bare walls, unless they have been prudent enough to provide themselves with tents and other paraphernalia of exploration.

A FONDUK.

Fonduks. The place of resort for travelling natives everywhere in North Africa is the Fonduk, which consists of a number of rough rooms, provided with little or no furniture and affording little more than shelter to the wanderer. In the centre is a large courtyard, where a great many camels and a sprinkling of other animals are congregated. It is the general resort of all countrymen who have come to the town for the exchange of impressions and gossip. Whole caravans may sometimes be seen assembled there, and the camel-drivers are always ready to afford any information which may be sought. The owner of the Fonduk keeps the keys of all the rooms, and cases of loss or robbery are practically unknown there.

Vermin. Nearly every writer of books of travel revenges himself for what he has suffered from the native vermin by wearying and disgusting his readers with indelicate details. I feel, therefore, that the critics would for once find something wanting in my book if I did not gratify them with some reference to this subject. I do not, however, propose to give them the benefit of my personal experiences, as I have always found insect-powder a sufficient prophylactic. It must, however, be mentioned for the benefit of intending travellers that all possible precautions are advisable. The British Vice-Consul at Susa told me that at one place in the interior the fleas had been so numerous that they had actually carried off his mattress from under him and deposited it upon the floor. But this I suspect must have been a consular report, if not an exaggeration. The precaution taken by Arabs against vermin is to place an oil night-light under the bed, and I am assured that this is an infallible attraction. A Frenchman who adopted this plan found that no less than eighty fleas had fallen victims in the course of one night.

Fantasias Whenever the occasion presents itself, a fantasia should be witnessed. The horses have the richest saddles of red velvet, embroidered with silver or gold, and, over their hind legs, a kind of long silk petticoat with copper sleigh-bells. The rider wears a sugar-loaf cap with ostrich feathers, a waistcoat and vest of yellow brocaded silk, and the brightest possible red

A COOK SHOP IN TUNIS.
(*Photograph by Mrs. Vivian.*)

leather boots. Every kind of evolution is executed, from quadrilles to tent-pegging and picking up handkerchiefs, while guns are fired in the air with much unnecessary noise. A favourite performance is that of carrying off a bride, while the simulation of the death of a horse and the combat between a horseman and a foot soldier are also very interesting.

An excellent fantasia was executed at Susa on the occasion of the last spring races.

Art. Arab pictorial art is delightful. It recalls children's drawings done by a first-class artist—say highly-coloured versions of Edward Lear's nonsense books. On the wall of a private house I saw a delightfully fantastic painting of an eagle carrying off a despondent donkey, whose tongue lolled out of his mouth and whose eye seemed to be inquiring whether the whole thing were not a huge joke. Then there was a very fat Arab on a tiny

ARAB ART.

little horse, proceeding at the rate of two miles an hour and evidently quite confident of being able to catch the exceedingly fleet ostrich he was chasing. There was also a mosque perched upon the top of a hill no larger than itself, and the hill was pierced by a tunnel, where a toy train was about to enter. The Arabs are very fond of making pictures of trains in all sorts of fanciful colours, and I have also seen wonderful representations of bicycles and French soldiers painted up on the walls of wayside coffee-houses.

Bicycles. The Arabs are all very fond of bicycles, which they call "the chariots of the winds." Riders in Tunisia always find that the whole population of a village turns out to admire them. The great attraction is that bicycles "don't eat barley," and nearly every Arab would have one if he could buy it as cheaply as a horse, say for £4 or £5.

A WAYSIDE TAVERN.
(*Photograph by* Mrs. Vivian.)

Of the motor-car he has a superstitious dread, and dubs it "the daughter of the devil."

An Itinerary. Travellers who intend to pursue their investigations beyond the town of Tunis will be glad of an itinerary, and I cannot do better than reproduce the one which I mapped out with the advice of the Residency, though in the event I was not encouraged to see it through.

Leave Tunis by the afternoon train and reach Susa at 9.50 p.m. You can see all there is to be seen at Susa in the course of the next morning, and, leaving at 12.18 p.m., you reach Kairwân at 2.40. I spent a week there, but a night or two will suffice for most people. If you can secure a decent carriage, you may drive on to El-Jem and Sfax, but it will probably be preferable to return to Susa and take your carriage there. If you have time to spare at Sfax, may you make an excursion to the Kerkenna Islands and inspect the fisheries. At Sfax take the Italian boat for Gabes, where a week may be pleasantly passed. Thence, if you are prepared to rough it, may you proceed to the Matmata plateau, Dwirat, Tatawin, and as far south as the military authorities will permit. Return by Mednin, Zarzis, and the island of Jerba to Gabes. Thence, if the Salt Lake is fordable, to Tozer and Nefta, whence you may make your way to the Algerian railway by Gafsa, Feriana, Kasserin, Sbeitla, Thala, Maktar, the battlefield of Zama, and El-Kef. From the railway you may make excursions to Beja and the valley of the Mejerda, to Tebursuk and the ruins of Dugga, before you return. With shorter excursions to Zaghwan, Hammamet and Nabeul, as well as to Bizerta and the forests of the Mogods, you will have obtained a fairly exhaustive impression of the whole of Tunisia.

Tunis to Susa. The narrow-gauge railway from Tunis to Susa is perhaps smoother and more comfortable than the others in the Regency; but time is evidently of very small moment, for the stoppages at wayside huts are long and frequent. Still, this is no great grievance, for the scenery is agreeable. The soil would appear to be poor, but it gladdens the eye with a rich carpet of wild flowers. The line is bordered at intervals with forests of laburnum, tufts of yellow ranunculus, giant orange hemlocks, brilliant broom, and delicate mauve asphodels, while the

SUSA: THE TRAMWAY TERMINUS FOR KAIRWÂN.
(*Photograph by Mrs. Vivian.*)

meadows are a kaleidoscope of colours, and young cornfields, bejewelled with fiery poppies, stretch away towards mysterious hills dotted with glistening villages. To the right is a well-kept road, where processions of disdainful camels and Liliputian donkeys lounge in long files; to the left, a turgid green sea, where shoals of small boats bob among the breakers.

KAIRWĀN.

Susa. Susa is a dismal little port, which is only visited as a stepping-stone for Kairwân. The only impressions Susa has left on my memory are of a long white wall with an outer boulevard beside an unsavoury sea, and of a raging, dusty wind, said to be almost chronic.

Susa to Kairwân. I was probably one of the last travellers to drive to Kairwân. There is an horse tramway, which covers the distance of forty miles in five or six hours; but it is so inconveniently crowded that most people prefer to go by carriage, which, with three fast horses, covers the ground nearly as fast. The ruts and wind were vastly disagreeable, but the panorama over the endless moor, which stretched away in every direction like an ocean of purple and green, was unique. Black *gurbis* and white flocks varied the landscape, and the silhouettes of gaunt camels on the horizon added an element of fantasy. The air of Kairwân is exhilarating, and I can well believe that it is even healthier than that of Tunis. As the European quarter is outside the walls, we may hope with confidence that the Holy City will long retain her old distinctive charm, and that the mania for building boulevards and imposing a dreadful modern symmetry will not accompany the new railway from Tunis.

Kairwân. After spending a week in the Holy City, I came away with a certain feeling of disenchantment. The chief impression is of poverty and squalor. The bright, particular vestments which gladden every street in Tunis are replaced in Kairwân by dingy rags, or, in the case of the better-to-do, by garments of dull brown, while the women are shrouded from head to foot in black wool. The perennial gaiety of Tunis is absent. Men stalk silently through the narrow streets, and, even when they haggle in the bazaars, there is always a note of irritation in their strident voices. Had I not been told so often that all Tunisia is satisfied with the present dispensation, I should have concluded that the Holy City was in mourning for the Rumi occupation.

In one sense the compulsory opening of the mosques has produced a greater tolerance of Christians, who may go anywhere in the town by night or day without encountering any expression of hostility. But who can say how far the hostility may not lurk beneath the surface? At most of the mosques I met with courtesy, though scarcely cordiality; while at the famous Mosque of the Barber, outside the walls, I was clearly shown that my presence was unwelcome. First a demand was made that I should take off my boots, and it was only when the guide had unblushingly alleged sore feet that I was grudgingly admitted, though the courtyard was provided with planks for visitors, and no such requirement had ever been made in any other mosque in Kairwán or Stambúl. After this everything was exhibited with sulky reluctance and much unnecessary expostulation lest I should intrude an inch too far. This and the Great Mosque have fine courtyards, some exquisite tiles, and woodwork of considerable antiquity; but otherwise the traveller might readily acquiesce in the closing of the

KAIKWAN: THE MAIN STREET.

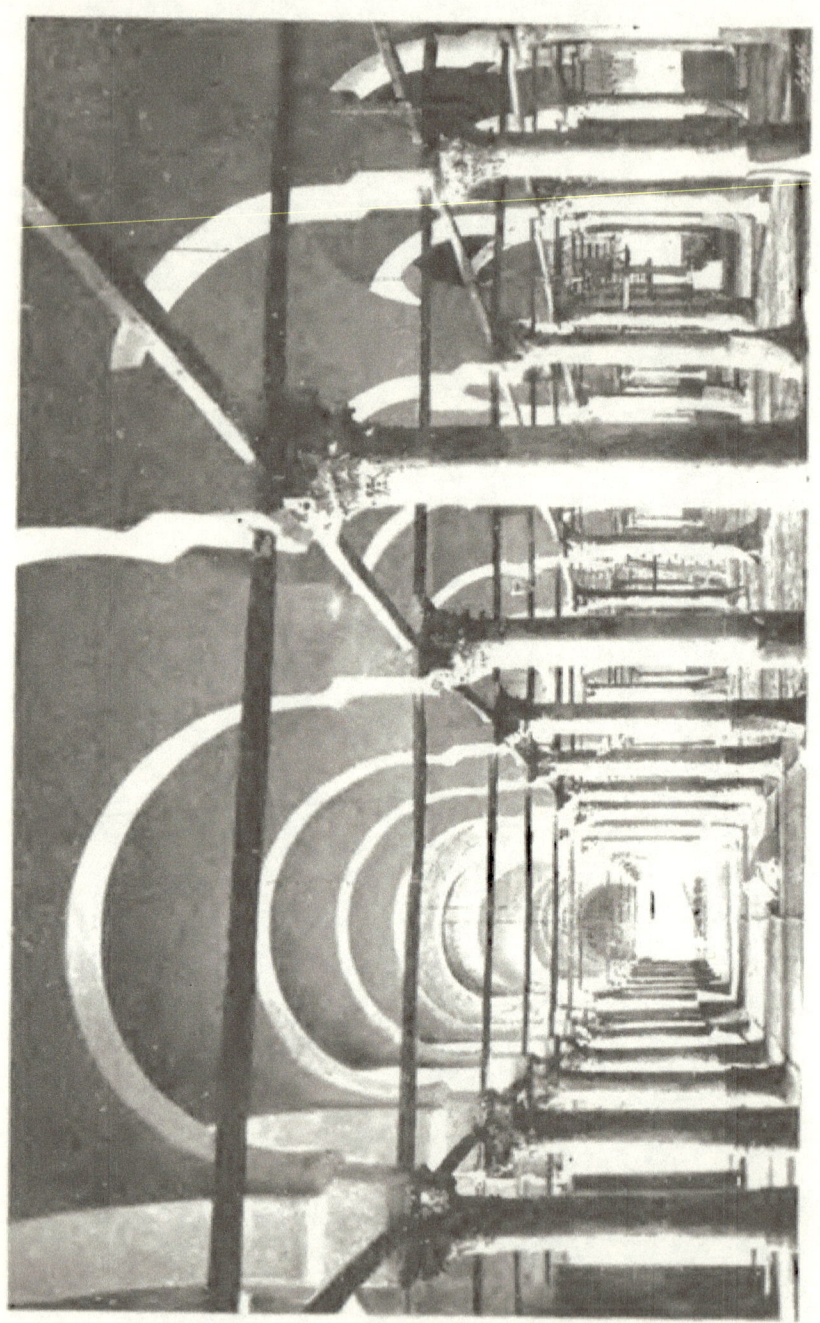

KAIRWÂN: INTERIOR OF THE GREAT MOSQUE.

mosques of Kairwân equally with those of the rest of Tunisia. At Kairwân they are plain, low buildings, crowded with coarse columns; they have no galleries, rich carpets, or Koranic shields, as at Stambûl, and the general impression is quite the reverse of magnificent.

Beside the mosques and the weekly performance of the Aïssawas there is positively nothing to attract the traveller to Kairwân. Had the railway been open, I should certainly not have remained so long. But, as it was, I found Kairwân, like Mecca or Siberia or the camp of the Khalifa, far easier to reach than to leave. The tramway is not only uncomfortable, but it is so inadequate in its accommodation that places cannot easily be secured, and there is no provision for hiring carriages. The only solace during enforced lingering at Kairwân was to wander about in search of quaint corners and street scenes. Here the little Mosque of the Three Doors, carved with ever dainty Arabic characters over the whole front; there a piteous group of camels being smeared all over with tar, and lifting up a mew-like complaint the while; yonder a madman, with a reputation for sanctity, gibbering and pointing a foolish finger at those who passed; again, a pretty market, freshly green, with crowds of sack-like purchasers grovelling on all fours about the various wares spread out upon the ground; and at every turn a row of butchers' booths, where impassive vendors plied esparto-whisks in a vain endeavour to chase myriads of flies from the array of unappetizing meat. This meat is always hung well outside the booths, and wayfarers must be wary to avoid frequent collision with it. It costs but 2½d. the lb., and is as unpalatable as it is throughout the Regency.

Perhaps the most amusing sight at Kairwân was that of the local aristocracy—the wives of the *contrôleurs* and other officials—clad in French provincial fashions of bygone years, assembled in a sandy public place where several roads meet, attempting to play croquet with tiny balls and prodigious hoops for the edification of countless ragged urchins. What a sign-manual of European civilization!

Sabra. In a great sunburnt plain about a mile to the south of Kairwân I made a pilgrimage to a great solitary stone, which has a romantic history, and may be regarded as a melancholy emblem of the present position of Islam. "It is *merabût*, a holy thing," said the Arab who accompanied me, as he bent his head in homage to the sanctity of the relic. It is the last survivor of the great city of Sabra, which in the 10th century was the equal, in size as well as in sanctity, of Kairwân herself. Sabra contained no less than three thousand baths attached to private houses, besides a goodly number of public bathing establishments; she possessed five gates, at the entrance of each one of which dues to the value of over £400 were levied every day. She was surnamed *El-Mansoura*, the victorious; but this name availed her little, for by the middle of the 12th century she was uninhabited, and now, but for this one remaining stone, her very site would be disputed. The whole of the rest of the town has been carried

away for building purposes in every direction, many of the pillars having been appropriated for the mosques of Kairwân. The legend, which explains the sparing of this remnant, is that the despoilers, finding it too heavy to carry off entire, began to saw it, whereupon it emitted a fearful groan, and blood began to trickle from its wound. This was a clear proof of the sanctity of the stone and the desire of

SABRA.
(Photograph by Mr. A Viccars.)

the immortals that it should not be removed; so here it remains, with its great blood-stained gash in the variegated marble, waiting for the day when Islam shall triumph once more, and Sabra, the victorious, may be built again with all her ancient splendour.

Susa to Sfax. The plain near Susa is remarkable for the greatest display of wild flowers I have ever beheld. They may for the most part be classified as weeds, but that does not detract from their profusion of colouring or the luxury of their scents. Here is an acre of dazzling poppies; there an hectare of tiny blossoms of the deepest blue, recalling the Ægean at noontide; yonder, an endless expanse of gold-red marigolds shimmering away to the horizon; and on all hands patches of wild mignonette with a

EL-JEM AMPHITHEATRE.

honeyed perfume, and strange purple thistles sweeter than triple heliotrope. Villages are few and far between, and the austerity of their windowless walls is almost forbidding.

El-Jem. The half-way stopping-place is at El-Jem, whose amphitheatre comes next to the Coliseum in size, and is superior to it in preservation. It describes a vast ellipse, over 160 yards across; but its chief use at present seems to be as a receptacle for all the garbage of the neighbourhood, and no attempt has been made to render the exploration of its galleries either safe or agreeable, nor is there anything to prevent the Arabs from carrying away stones for building material, as they have been accustomed to do for generations. The schoolmaster is bound to put up travellers, who may rely on monastic accommodation and good plain fare at hotel prices.

The journey on is through an even drearier plain until the approach to Sfax and its seven thousand gardens. For my part, if I were advising a friend of mine, I would bid him buy photographs of El-Jem Amphitheatre in Tunis, and proceed from Tunis to Sfax (if, indeed, he must go there) by boat.

Sfax. By the time I had reached Sfax, I had come reluctantly to the conclusion that, under present conditions, travel in the interior is almost out of the question. Apart from the trouble of buying horses, tents, provisions, and other concomitants of exploration, it would not be agreeable to stray far from our consulates under the evil eye of suspicious officials, who might at any time be driven to arbitrary action through excess of zeal. It would be so easy to arrest an inconvenient wanderer on a pretext of espionage, and a tardy release would be but imperfect redress. But I do not hesitate to recommend the journey along the coast, which offers a series of fascinating scenes at the cost of little discomfort.

Sfax pleased me vastly. It is not alluring from the sea, presenting only an array of tawdry European houses straggling over a sandy waste. But the old Arab town, with its jagged Saracen wall, its narrow lanes, through none of which a carriage can pass, its varied street scenes, its fantastic balconies,

SFAX: MARKET OUTSIDE THE WALLS.
(*Photograph by* Mrs. Vivian.)

its wonderful green gateways, and its strange arched bazaars, is a constant delight. At Susa and Kairwân the dinginess of the drab costumes contributed to a depressing impression, but at Sfax the urchins were brilliantly polychrome. The outlines of the town were not so soft as at Tunis, but they were far more brilliantly cheerful, and harmonized with the dazzling sun on the white-washed walls. Many children wore parti-coloured cloths, the right half scarlet and the left half Cambridge blue, or one side purple and the other salmon pink, like glorified clowns. The men wore gigantic turbans, mostly green, which implies a claim to descent from the Prophet, and they conveyed an air of festivity by the large pink roses or geraniums poised behind their ears. I recognised many types of face which were familiar to me from the *Arabian Nights*, and more than one sea-dog who was certainly a pirate in the good old times. Sfax is perhaps best known in France from its association with the various notorieties of the Zola case. The best house in the town is pointed out as having been the abode of Esterhazy, and it is amusing to note that the principal shop is kept by a man named Dreyfus. The Greek fishermen are so important a colony there that many of the coffee-houses bear the word Ξενοδοχεῖον and other inscriptions in the Hellenic character.

Fortifications. Encouraged by the acquiescence of Europe in the fortification of Bizerta, the French Government is now about to turn Sfax into a military and naval stronghold. Unlike Bizerta, which possesses the disadvantages of being easily blockaded, Sfax will make an excellent naval station. The islands of Kerkenna supply it with a natural rampart, as well as easy outlets to the north and south. Its position constitutes it an answer, if not a menace, to Malta; and we may here, perhaps for the first time, feel anxiety at the presence of the French in Tunisia. On the 22nd of March, 1898, a tender was accepted for the construction of barracks to accommodate ninety sailors, as well as powder and torpedo magazines. The present expenditure is £3,200, and the works are to begin at once. The intention is to follow them up with far more extensive fortifications later on.

BREAD-STALL IN THE OASIS OF GABES.
(*Photograph by* Mrs. Vivian.)

Gabes. The land journey from Sfax to Gabes is over such bad roads and so desolate a tract of country that it is wiser to go by sea. The Italian service of boats is well appointed, but if the weather be bad, many might resent the trial of spending eight hours at anchor outside the canal which leads to the

THE INSIDE OF THE CUP AND THE PLATTER 215

harbour of Sfax, and the landing at Gabes by means of small boats a mile away from shore.

I really think I prefer Gabes to any other place in Tunisia. It consists of a cluster of poor houses built to

OASIS OF GABES: INTERIOR OF A HOUSE

minister to the wants of the French garrison, and a tropical array of palm trees of every size. There are delightful gardens, where pomegranates, bananas, bamboos, and many luxuriant flowers abound. And the Arab villages of the oasis are as surprising by their architecture as by their hospitality. I traversed strange underground streets of exceeding darkness, flanked by boulders which might well puzzle an archæologist. Some were well-formed capitals of columns, like those of the walls of El-Jem amphitheatre; others were megalithons furnished with round holes, such as have been rashly identified with Baal-worship in Tripoli. Nearly all were full of fossils. The streets were so low that I had to stoop frequently as I walked, but I was told that camels can and do pass through them. Most of the houses are built on two stories—the lower a mere courtyard with cattle-sheds, the upper a rude terrace with adjoining hovels for the families. Where wood is necessary, planks of palm trees are generally used with reckless extravagance.

The Arabs of the interior do not veil or mew up their women, and I was allowed to enter freely into every house. I was made welcome with many polite speeches, and excited quite as much curiosity as I experienced. Two missionary ladies who accompanied the party aroused much astonishment by confessing they were unmarried, and surprise was expressed that I did not add them to my harem. I was much commiserated for the shortcomings of my Arabic, and told that any one who spoke no Arabic might as well be dumb. The women had tattoo marks on their chins in the shape of an imperial, a light tattoo mark on the tips of their noses, rows of little pigtails matted over their foreheads, and every variety of amulet, from the ubiquitous "hand of Fatima" to

THE INSIDE OF THE CUP AND THE PLATTER 217

rosaries of coloured glass and long leather cases containing spells against serpents. I was dismissed with many blessings and pats on the back, my hostess remarking that all strangers were good people, save only the Jews, who were all rascals.

At Gabes nearly every one is a gardener, and everything is subservient to the question of irri-

the oasis at its present state of prosperity, whereas the neighbouring oasis of Hamma has almost ceased to exist owing to the reckless waste of water.

Gabes is probably, from the agricultural point of view, one of the most prosperous parts of Tunisia, land fetching as much as £300 per acre, and property is extremely subdivided. The beehives there are worth noting. They are roughly constructed with old drain pipes, but they succeed in producing excellent honey. The bee in favour there is a large black variety, which I have never seen anywhere else.

To appreciate Gabes fully I think one ought to arrive there from the interior. After a long period of thirst and scorching heat, the sight of green trees and bubbling brooks on every hand makes it easy to understand that the Arab should have chosen a garden as his vision of paradise. But coming there from anywhere, it is impossible not to be captivated by the charming scene. Here Nature wears her most luxuriant aspect; and there can be no more soothing and agreeable experience than wandering for hours along little paths under the palm trees, with fragrant shrubs and lovely flowers ministering to every craving of the senses.

A Sandstorm. My enjoyment of Tunis was somewhat tempered by almost incessant rain, and at Gabes I found that sand storms are frequent at all times of the year. When I awoke one morning, I found the whole courtyard of the inn dense with whirling clouds of sand, and the boots I had put out were almost buried in a drift. The sand had come in through window cracks, and my clothes suggested that I must have rolled them in the desert. When I went out, I could scarcely see across the street, and, after fighting my way some twenty yards to the post office, I found my whole body coated with sand, which had penetrated inside my boots, collar, nose, mouth, and ears. Though the wind was strong, the air was of the most oppressive weight and recalled the inside of a hot-house. A drive in the afternoon across a stretch of desert to a neighbouring oasis was one of the most disagreeable experiences I ever endured. At the end of five minutes I was so hopelessly blinded and drenched with sand that I was almost fain to sigh for the streaming skies of Tunis.

Wells. One of the strangest sights in the oases is that of a caravan or a herd reaching the wells after a long desert journey. The animals know that their thirst is at length to be quenched, and it requires infinite pains and patience to prevent them from rushing forward and injuring themselves, in their wild efforts to come first. As a rule a rough pen is erected, and they are only let out to the water ten or twelve at a time, an operation which requires great strength and force of character on the part of the drovers.

Jerba. The Island of the Lotus or Date Eaters contains no towns, but merely an agglomeration of villages, of which Humt Suk is considered the capital. On the boat I entered into conversation with a shabby-looking young Frenchman, who told me with a grand air that he was the Governor of the Island. I imagine he was merely the *contrôleur civil*, or French prefect. It was at Humt Suk that a tower of skulls was erected in 1560, after the defeat of the Spaniards by Dragut Pasha. It was described in 1832 as being twenty feet high and ten feet at the base, tapering toward the top, and composed of alter-

A WAYSIDE WELL BETWEEN EL-JEM AND SFAX.
(*Photograph by Mrs. Vivian.*)

nate layers of skulls and bones. In 1848 the Bey of Tunis acceded to a request of the European Consuls, and the remains were buried in the Christian cemetery of Jerba. This was a favourite form of monument in the middle ages, and it is strange that it should not have survived more often. The Montenegrins were fond of making similar trophies with the bones of their enemies, and, when I was in Servia, I noted the indignation with which the people of Nish looked upon the remains of a tower which the Turks had made there early in the century.

There is still an imposing Spanish fort at Humt Suk, which, though it cannot compare with the Spanish fort at Tripoli, is yet in very good preservation. Nearly the whole European population of Jerba is now Maltese. The Jerbians themselves differ considerably in appearance, habits, and religion from the Arabs of the neighbouring mainland. They are looked upon as heretics by orthodox Muhammadans, and are divided into a number of sects which regard each other as heretics. There are many traces of paganism in the Muhammadanism of Jerba, where a great many households set up a shrine and place upon it offerings and libations to the household god. Some people are of opinion that this is a form of devil worship, and the Jerbians are certainly very averse from speaking about it. The mosques in the island are readily shown to strangers, though there is no compulsion about it as at Kairwân.

The passage from Jerba to the mainland is a very narrow one and so shallow that there is no difficulty about wading across it at low tide. It is a curious fact that, while the Mediterranean is tideless, its big recesses, the Adriatic and the Gulf of Gabes, have very decided tides.

There probably remained at Jerba a greater proportion of the original native race than anywhere else in Tunisia; for the various conquests which passed over the land seem to have left a fainter imprint upon this favoured island. The language there contains a greater element of Berber roots and is more closely connected with the speech of Rhadames than with that of Tunis. Many industries are also the same as at Rhadames. The woollen garments are almost identical. The islanders have always excelled in commerce, and many of the most prosperous merchants in Tunis are recruited from among them. Their pottery is second only to that of Nabeul. They shave their beards, which is unusual among the Arabs of the interior. Many of the men wear large hats, like a caricature of Buffalo Bill, and the women pointed caps or the sugar-loaf pattern.

The importance of Jerba is that it affords a warehouse for the whole of the south of Tunisia. At present the boats have to anchor several miles away, but no doubt in process of time steps will be taken to provide a place with a fortified harbour. Nor is it impossible that, if the French ever obtain the control of the caravan trade with the interior, they may succeed in turning Jerba into one of the principal ports of the desert.

Sbeitla. The old town of Sbeitla stands upon a plateau, overlooking the Wed Sbeitla, which issues from a wild gorge a little way off to the North West. A great many centuries ago it was the capital of a kingdom, and it has figured prominently in the annals of Tunisia throughout the dark ages. Now only the temples and triumphal arches—without which no Roman town was complete—have survived, and the presence of a few cattle browsing among their ruins may be taken as a fair type of the degeneracy of the whole land. The remains of the town itself present so hopelessly confused a mass that at present it is impossible to make head or tail of it; and unless the French make a radical change in their archæological policy it is likely to remain so.

The chief, indeed the only, interest accessible to the passing traveller is to be found in the three famous temples which stand side by side, and the triumphal arch, decorated with four Corinthian columns and bearing inscriptions of the 2nd century. The middle temple is of a composite style, the other two are Corinthian. Passing through the triumphal arch, you find a broad way paved with large flag stones, which, despite the wear and tear of centuries, look as if they might have been put down yesterday. Diligent research in the neighbourhood has evolved certain conjectural theories as to the site of a theatre and amphitheatre; but until serious excavations shall be undertaken in a business-like way, it is impossible to form any positive opinion as to anything here.

Thala. The present Arab village of Thala is probably not the Thala of Jugurtha, unless the configuration of the neighbourhood has changed completely since the days of Sallust. It consists of a few irregular, tumble-down houses, huddled together at the bottom of a narrow valley. There are ruins everywhere, only waiting to be dug up; but we might say as much of almost any spot taken at random in the Regency. This by no means proves that we have found the original Thala, a word which in the Berber language means a spring; in Arabic is given to a gum-tree, and is therefore by no means uncommon.

Some French travellers who visited Thala soon after the occupation, relate an incident which occurred to them there and serves to show the French attitude towards the natives. They were entertained by an unfortunate merchant of the locality, and, with the assistance of a servile kaïd, proceeded to give him an uncomfortable quarter of an hour as a return for his hospitality. They began by telling him that they had heard of his fighting against the French, and intended to hand him over to the military authorities, whereupon he grovelled upon the ground, kissed the hem of their garments, swore his devotion to France, and implored for mercy. "It is idle to protest," said the kaïd, "unless you give some proof of your devotion. You must put on European dress." "But I cannot thus go against the laws of my religion," he pleaded. "It is your only hope of escape." "Very well, if there is nothing else for it, give me a hat, and I will wear it, even though I imperil my soul." He accordingly put on one of the Frenchmen's travel-stained hats. But this was not enough. "Now to complete the test," said the kaïd, "and show these gentlemen once for all what sacrifices you are prepared to make for them, you must lend them your wife." The poor man then burst into a torrent of piteous lamentations. "My wife! ah, no! That is impossible," he cried; "but I will give them my mother-in-law, my sister-in-law, all the members of my wife's family if they like. For God's sake let their lordships be content, and take away my mother-in-law with them." The scene was protracted for a long time, to the huge diversion of the Frenchmen, and eventually they wound it up by tearing off several of the poor wretch's clothes and driving him away with violent blows on his back and his head, roaring with inextinguishable laughter as they followed up each blow with a tremendous kick. And yet they express surprise that the French have not contrived to make themselves popular among the Arabs.

El-Kef. The rock of El-Kef recalls that of Constantine in Algeria, or an ogre's castle in a dream. Its ramparts, battlements and barbicans are so wedded to the natural rock that, until you are actually there, it is impossible to make sure how much is due to nature and how much to art. The very houses which crouch upon the side suggest limpet constructions begotten of the rock itself. You are here in a wild country, where every face seems to scowl at you, and where you feel that if the natives were not for the moment overawed, you would have a short shrift. As usual, nature is in tune with the temperament of the natives, and the rough road, guarded by inhospitable rocks, the frowning sands, the ungenerous vegetation, seem to emit a constant protest against your intrusion. On a rainy day the precipitous streets are like mountain torrents, in which you are almost washed away, and during the hot weather the dust is so great that you might almost fancy yourself in the thick of a sand-storm.

The town was dedicated to Venus by the Carthaginians, who used to exile their revolted mercenaries thither, as every one who has read Flaubert's *Salambo* will remember. It is still an important Arab town, and many sects and secret societies have taken refuge there, in the hope of being less interfered with than they would be in Tunis. It is one of the few towns of the interior which have given any sign of reviving since the occupation; but one result, disappointing to archæologists, is that many of the ancient remains have been appropriated for modern building. The only trace remaining of the ancient worship of Venus there is the habit of the Arabs to offer doves, in fulfilment of vows, at a mosque which has been thought to occupy the site of the ancient temple. There are twelve Roman cisterns, among the finest in the world, and second only to those of Carthage. A short distance outside the town an amphitheatre and a theatre with Ionic columns may be traced. There are two Byzantine churches, which would not require any very great effort to restore. A branch line to El-Kef has often been talked of, but it will probably be a long time before any attempt at a complete railway system is made in Tunisia, and the town may hope to preserve something of its natural charm for a good while yet.

Beja. Beja stands on the slope of a hill amid white ramparts and silvery olive trees. It was

THE INSIDE OF THE CUP AND THE PLATTER

an important city at the time of Hannibal's wars, and had a reputation for riches and fertility at the zenith of Arab rule. It is scarcely too much to say that Beja has continued, from the days of Sallust to our own, the most important grain market in North Africa. The mosque there is dedicated to Jesus Christ, who, as every one knows, is revered by the Muhammadans as one of their most holy *merabuts*. The old Byzantine wall, flanked by 22 towers, is still in very fair condition on three sides of the town. Some desultory excavations have revealed an extensive Carthaginian cemetery containing many skeletons, but very little else except some ordinary pottery, among which was a jar, which had evidently been broken before the funeral and mended again with iron wire.

The Mejerda. The valley of the Mejerda is of infinite fertility, but wears a forbidding aspect. All the colours are sombre, and the river itself is a bilious torrent, which suggests an invading army rather than a bounteous benefactor. The chief river of Tunisia is in many ways typical of the Arab character. At times it slumbers along through an immense, fertile plain; then of a sudden it breaks away from all control, and carries away everything before it; bridges, houses, flocks and herds, are swept along like feathers in a tempest.

Dugga. Dugga is approached from Tebursuk by a picturesque path, which meanders among little hills and barley fields, protected against the birds by live scarecrows, who make a great noise, scream-

ing and cracking long leather thongs. Dugga
stands upon an abrupt hill, which serves as a
landmark from a long distance. It is but a very

DUGGA: CORINTHIAN TEMPLE.

unpretentious Arab village and only merits attention
for the sake of the adjoining ruins. Perhaps the most
interesting of them is the mausoleum, or rather

what remains of it,—the only known monument of architecture which has remained from Punic times. It formerly possessed an inscription in the Lybian and Punic tongues, which was of the utmost use in determining several characters of the Lybian alphabet. Sir Thomas Read, our Consul at Tunis, carried it off to the British Museum and, unfortunately, the Arabs, whom he employed to do this, pulled down the upper part of the mausoleum in order to facilitate their work. A picture taken in 1832 represents the mausoleum as being then still in a fairly perfect condition.

There are also a theatre, with 25 rows of steps, and the frontage of a Corinthian temple, dedicated to Marcus Aurelius and Lucius Verus, with an exquisitely sculptured cornice and nearly perfect capitals. Standing on the top of a hill, the temple dominates the whole neighbourhood and presents to the approaching traveller an exquisite outline, which is scarcely surpassed by that of the Acropolis at Athens. The steps were formerly surmounted by a wonderful portico, which must have commanded an ideal view over the gardens and olive yards, the rich villas and flourishing towns, stretching away to the purple mountains upon the horizon. The rest of the temple is now a confused ruin, but a perfunctory examination reveals exquisite mosaics, graceful columns, and rich carvings, which only await a little enterprise to offer an irresistible attraction to every traveller in the Regency.

Bizerta. The town, and particularly the harbour, of Bizerta have recently assumed a wholly fictitious importance. When the French took over Tunisia, they promised not to fortify Bizerta, but, borrowing a leaf out of the book of their Russian ally, they are now laying themselves out to make it impregnable. They have built a fort behind the town, another on the adjoining heights, and have voted the money for six more in the neighbourhood.

There has lately been much unnecessary alarm over rumours of the cession of Bizerta to the Russians, and of an understanding that the Russian fleet shall be allowed to occupy the harbour in case of war. As a matter of fact, we might have had Bizerta ourselves forty or fifty years ago, but our naval authorities rightly judged that it was not worth troubling about. To begin with, Bizerta does not command any important position, and has no particular use as a coaling station.

Stress is laid upon the fact that all the fleets of the world might easily be concealed there, and, awaiting their opportunity, might sally forth and command the Mediterranean. The old harbour was modest enough, and the French have now cut a channel into the great salt lake behind the town, which lake, equal in area to the whole city of Paris, affords the largest harbour in the world. It is certainly an excellent lake, for it is full of delicious fish, which supply the market of Tunis and render a stay there a pleasure. But most naval experts are agreed that, though all the navies of the world may take refuge in the harbour, they will by no means find it so easy to come out again. A ship or two judiciously sunk at the entrance to the canal would "bottle up" the fleets for weeks or months.

Moreover, Bizerta, though it is to be so admirably defended by sea, is scarcely at all defended by land. It would suffice to land an army on the coast to the South and march on the place. Then the fleets, cooped up in the lake, would be at the mercy of the surrounding army; for their guns, being intended for use at a minimum range of half a mile, would be quite useless against ordinary artillery. To sum up, we may grumble at the French for breaking faith and fortifying a place they had undertaken not to fortify, though we should probably have done the same under similar circumstances. But we are free to confess that we have nothing to fear.

Bizerta is picturesque but dull. There is a charming quarter, still named "Andalusian," which was colonized by Moors on their expulsion from Spain. The descendants of these Moors are still distinct in habits and appearance from the Arabs in the other quarters of the town. At one time they were inveterate pirates, and they kept up a fierce fanaticism until very recent times. It is only quite lately that Christians or Jews have been allowed to set foot in their quarter.

As a modern residence, Bizerta suffers by the exigencies of military strategy. Particularly at this period of spy-mania, a visitor may scarcely venture anywhere, for he is warned off at every touch and turn from the approach to some military undertaking. Walking about with a guide, I came upon a board marked "*Défense d'entrer*" at the entrance to a fort, which is now used only as a barrack. I was for turning back, but the guide said, "Come on, it is all right." I had not proceeded many yards, however, before an officer came out of the fort at a great pace and marched down upon me. I began to regret that I had brought a camera, and cherished visions of the lock-up. However, the officer passed on with a polite bow, and I was suffered to climb an eminence and photograph at large. Still, there was a feeling of insecurity about the proceeding, and I do not hanker after residence at Bizerta.

The salt lake, for instance, would be very pleasant for boating, but the fishing has been taken over by a company, and no boat may venture to disturb it. The canal must also be a constant nuisance. In consideration of its having been dry land, the huge steam ferry, which must have cost a large sum to erect, is free to all comers. Horses, carriages, waggons, peasants, funerals, all huddle together on a kind of floating platform, and are slowly tugged across. Sometimes they must wait forty minutes or an hour for the ferry, if there be ships or other obstruction. Sometimes the rope breaks, and they drift helplessly down towards the open sea until a steam tug comes to tow them back. Then it will be three or four hours until the ferry is re-established, and you may lose your temper if you are driving out to dinner or to catch a train.

Bizerta is connected with Tunis by a ramshackle light railway, which takes over three hours to cover

THE INSIDE OF THE CUP AND THE PLATTER 233

thirty-six miles. It is far pleasanter to charter a pair of strong mules and drive over in four and a half hours. Until the end of January, 1898, there was an excellent hotel in Bizerta, better than any in

BIZERTA FERRY: PASSAGE OF A FUNERAL.
(Note basket containing baby's corpse on the right.)
(Photograph by M.. Vivian.)

Tunis. It was kept by a French gentleman. He had bought it as a private house, and, losing his money, tried in vain to let it. Then he decided to open it as an hotel; but so few people come to Bizerta, and those so poor, that he was soon compelled to put up his shutters. Now, however, I hear that it has been reopened under good management, and it should prosper since the mail steamers have taken to touching at Bizerta. With a little effort, it may soon become a tourist resort on a small scale, and we may live to see a casino facing its silver sands.

A recent incident at Bizerta deserves to be mentioned as an illustration of the present temper of the French towards us. The day before the arrival of the French fleet for their annual manœuvres, a British vessel, bound from India to Southampton, arrived off this harbour with the intention of coaling, but was informed that as India was infected with plague, she must wait outside and coal there. She accordingly sought out the best anchorage she could find, and in the process contrived to run aground at a spot which completely blocked the entrance to the harbour. If the French fleet had then been inside, it would have been as effectively "bottled up" as that of Admiral Cervera by the *Merrimac*. As it was, if our ship remained there, the French fleet, which was expected on the morrow, would not have been able to come in, and onlookers would have been provided with excellent ocular demonstration of the uselessness of the harbour of Bizerta, upon which the French pride themselves so vastly. Naturally the French were furious. They declared that they had positive information of the presence of a notorious spy on board, and that the British ship had run aground on purpose; as if so great a sacrifice would have been worth making to obtain information which is easily accessible to every traveller who cares to keep his eyes open. At first a serious demand was made that the ship should be blown up, but at length more prudent counsels prevailed, and she was easily towed off. Angry denunciations of English perfidy are still, however, maintained in the Tunisian press, and the locality does not even solace itself with the reflection that our ship's visit to this hospitable port involved it in an expenditure of nearly £500. Such incidents as this, coupled with the difficulties which are constantly being placed in the path of travellers in Tunisia, are not likely to facilitate the development of the country as a tourist resort, which the authorities of the Regency constantly profess to have at heart.

Chapter VIII

TRADE AND AGRICULTURE

Vulture-Princes—Bazaars—Industries—Saddlery — Sheshias— Dyeing — Tanners—Carpets—Perfumes—Arms—Potteries—Halfagrass — Trade with the interior — Rhadames — Rhat— The Tuaregs—Agricultural Methods — Habbus — Wells —The Cactus — Vines—Olives—Fisheries—Sponges—Pulps.

Vulture-Princes. It is perhaps chiefly for their bazaars that Arab towns entrance the traveller. You may come to know every detail of Arab life and habits and you may satiate yourself with the vivid local colour, but assuredly you must be hard to please if you ever tire of the infinite variety of the bazaars. You must, however, set out with a plentiful stock of patience, for hurry is unknown in the East, and there are armies of pertinacious touts, who pounce upon the stranger on the instant of his arrival, and are almost impossible to shake off. As the merchants never leave their shops, and even require some persuasion before bestirring themselves to serve a customer, they rely almost entirely upon the hotel guides and their own touts. A tout never confesses what he is, but accosts you with a specious invitation to visit his shop or his uncle's, as the case may be. Then he leads you to his employers and proceeds to pull down all the wares and display them as if they were his own. The merchants are made to fetch and carry for him and bidden bring you coffee. He will bring down a piece of stuff worth at the outside 20 francs and coolly ask you 200 for it. If you are new to the game, you will think yourself very clever in getting it for 150, and later on in the day he will return to the merchant to divide the profit. If you fail to find what you require in the first shop, he will take you to another, describing it as his branch establishment, and you will probably be taken in by the deference shown him by the real proprietor, who is of course in the swim. If you wish to choose your own design, he will take you to the small factories, where every man works for himself, and inform you with a lordly air "Here are our workpeople." These touts often grow very rich, as it is by no means unusual for an American to come and spend £400 for things which may be worth forty, and this leaves a good deal to be divided up. As there is absolutely no price in the bazaars, save what may be decided by shameless bargaining, neither is there any limit to the extortion which may be practised on those who are ignorant of the value of Oriental goods.

The touts are to be met with anywhere or everywhere. In your hotel dining-room, outside a coffeehouse, or in the seat next to you at the theatre, you may find a gorgeous Oriental, who falls into conversation with you and tells you all manner of interesting things. In the end he pulls out his card, and informs you that he is one of the principal merchants in the bazaars, and that if you will come to his shop he hopes that you will look upon it as your home. If you come at a time when he is expecting you, you will find him awaiting you in state, with all the people at his beck and call, but if you chance to come at an inconvenient season, you may discover him in his shirt sleeves measuring a nigger for a livery. Most of these touts have from time to time done something to put themselves within the meshes of the law, and have suffered various terms of imprisonment; but no decisive action has ever yet been taken against them, unless we except a recent occasion, when a party of some 200 tourists was in possession of the town, and the Government arbitrarily shut up all the touts for twenty-four hours until the departure of the tourists.

These touts have been happily dubbed "vultures" by a local paper. A particularly persistent "vulture," the hero of a thousand impudent exploits, recently acquired considerable notoriety by his prowess in passing himself off on an English yachtsman as the Bey's son. He once went to Malta, and was received everywhere in society and at officers' clubs and messes as a Tunisian prince.

Bazaars. The bazaars at Tunis are said to be the best in Africa, if not in the Orient, bearing comparison even with those of Stambúl. I think they now subsist to a large extent on a worn-out reputation, but there are still wonderful embroideries, carpets from Kairwán, woven silks, and cloth of the

subtlest shades to be found at reasonable prices.
Of course, many goods are of French manufacture;
but they are made for the African market and could
not be bought in Europe at any price, so that they
acquire an Oriental character, like Asiatic idols
made, but not to be purchased, in Birmingham. The
best native embroideries are generally worked on
the commonest material, the merchants explaining
this on the score of durability. As labour is cheap
in Tunis, their intrinsic value is low; and as each
merchant has his own looms, he is always ready to
weave any pattern a customer may order. The
process of purchase is generally long, necessitating
several hours' negotiation and the consumption of
an inordinate amount of coffee. Does a customer
spend a whole afternoon in seeing the shop turned
upside down, the utmost good nature prevails, even
though he decide to buy nothing. He is overwhelmed
with compliments, begged to consider the whole shop
as his own, and encouraged to come again, as if the
mere pleasure of his company were ample reward.
Should he decide on a purchase, every franc is contested mercilessly, but, once a bargain is concluded,
he is treated as a benefactor.

The favourite gag in the large shops is to tell you
that second-hand goods have either belonged to
the Bey, or to one of his generals, and this is a
fruitful pretext for enhancing the price. This is
of course almost always a romance. But it appears to be the fact that most of the big shops
employ a number of old women, who go the round

of the harems and buy up all the pretty old things they can find, or else give tawdry modern things in exchange for them. It is also usual to pretend that the carpets, arms, and embroideries come from

GUARD AT THE ENTRANCE OF THE BAZAARS.

Mecca, but this is very rarely true. Much merchandise comes from Syria, but most of what we find is made in Tunis or Kairwân.

The bazaars consist of whitewashed arcades with a

BAZAARS OF TUNIS.

number of niches where the smaller fry make or sell their goods, and regular shops where Jama'al and other merchant princes abide. At the back of Jama'al's shop is an open court with an orange tree in the middle and little rooms giving on to a gallery all round. This, he tells you, is the old slave-market and the human wares used to be lodged in these little rooms until they were sold. With the exception of the big shops, which are bazaars in our sense of the word and which contain a large variety of goods, the various trades are divided into streets, as used to be the wont in Europe.

Industries. Everything is mediæval in Tunisia, and it is not therefore surprising to find that all the artisans are constituted into guilds, each presided over by a master, called *amin*, who controls the admission of apprentices and takes care that all work is done according to traditional methods. The *amin* is elected by the members of his guild, subject to the ratification of the Bey. The principal guild is that of the makers of *sheshias*, and among others may be noted the dyers, saddle-makers, silk-weavers, locksmiths, perfumers, goldsmiths, masons, tanners, potters, hoopers, masseurs in the Moorish baths, and even the circumcisers.

Saddlery. The saddlers' bazaar is perhaps the most pleasing and highly-considered in Tunis. Any occupation remotely connected with horses acquires dignity there, and many of the better-class Arabs take a pleasure in apprenticing themselves for some years to a saddler. It is, moreover, in the

centre of this bazaar that one of the most famous of
the Tunisian saints has been buried. His tomb, a
wooden box brightly painted with green and red,
stands in the middle of the roadway, and all who
pass through on foot or on horseback must step aside
in deference to his memory. Where an Arab can
afford fine clothes for himself, he deems it doubly
necessary to provide handsome trappings for his
horse. Turquoises and other jewels are often used,
but silk and gold and silver thread, embroidered upon
every kind of coloured leather with all the imagination of Arab workmanship, are most usual. A
saddler works all his designs out of his head, according to tradition, and although the leather is nearly
all imported from France, there can be no doubt
about the Oriental character of the finished article.
The saddles are always elaborately worked, and
have, as a rule, a high back to them, which makes
riding, but not mounting, a luxury. The bridle is
also excessively decorated, and the trappings on
the horse's head are provided with all manner of
jingling adjuncts, which are considered of special
use against the evil eye. The bits are generally
decorated with metal crescents or ivory hands, for the
same purpose. You may also see in the shops
silver stirrups and spurs very richly damascened.
The saddler occupies his spare time in embroidering
fancy foot-stools, which you are expected to stuff
for yourself at home with horse-hair; little pocket
mirrors encased in leather; and pouches for containing charms.

THE ANGLERS' BAZAAR.

Sheshias. The Tunisian fez is narrower than the Turkish and has a much bigger tassel, of blue silk instead of black. In old days its manufacture was one of the chief industries of Tunis, but of late years the competition of inferior Austrian wares, at less than half the price, has caused great depression. The process is a simple one. The rudimentary cap is coarsely knitted in thick white wool, somewhat resembling that known as double Berlin. It then looks like a loose jelly-bag and is washed until it has shrunk considerably. After this it is teased with thistle combs, two of which are fixed together on a rude wooden frame. The fluffy surface is then shorn and the sheshia goes to Zaghwan to be dyed scarlet. The industry of sheshia-dyeing there used to be the staple one of the place, but it has now suffered severely from the foreign competition.

Dyeing. There are seventy dyeing establishments at Tunis, sixty-two at Sfax, twenty-five (Jews) at Jerba, ten at Kairwân, and many others elsewhere. Each place has its own system. For instance, at Susa an equal weight of dates is added to the indigo. The favourite dyes employed in Tunisia are indigo, cochineal, alizari, pomegranate flowers, gall nuts, and henna; but gradually, with French influence, inferior powdered dyes are coming in ready-prepared, and none of the colours now have anything approaching the permanency which they possessed before the occupation.

Tanning. Most of the bark used in tanning comes from the North of Tunisia, the favourite being that of the Aleppo pine. The skins are placed in huge jars, containing forty or fifty gallons, and, after being washed in salt water, are soaked in the various decoctions of bark. The tanneries at Kairwân were formerly of equal repute with those of Morocco, but though ten establishments still remain in the Holy City, the industry is far from prosperous. The favourite skins are those of sheep and goats, particularly for making shoe leather. The parchments, required for making books in a land where nothing is ephemeral, are prepared from sheep skins subjected to an epilatory process.

Carpets. Kairwân carpets enjoy a reputation all over the world, but, as seems to be the case with almost everything in this unfortunate country, their glory has departed. At present, 400 families in Kairwân produce carpets to the value of £10,000 or £11,000 a year. But prices are steadily going down —they have fallen from 12s. to 7s. 6d. the square yard during the last few years alone,—and it becomes a question how long it will be worth while to continue making carpets at all. Many, however, of great beauty and durability, may still be had, and their perfection is probably due, in a large measure, to the fact that their production has been, and still is, a home industry. No doubt French capitalists will presently establish factories on a large scale, and then the Holy City will degenerate into a sort of French Kidderminster. The carpets are, in almost every case, made by women, who crouch behind a clumsy frame and work, not only without a model, but even

BAZAARS OF TUNIS

without seeing what they are turning out. Each family has its own design, which is reproduced, with slight variations according to individual fancy, from

A CARPET WEAVER.

generation to generation. The most expensive carpets are a mixture of wool and cotton, requiring more labour than those entirely of wool. The size and shape of the carpets vary according as they are intended for prayer, for the backs of horses, or for the furnishing of tents. Elsewhere in the Regency very fair woollen carpets are reproduced, notably at Susa, at Jara in the oasis of Gabes, and among the nomadic Swassi. Silk coverings are woven at Jerba, and in the oasis of the Jerid ; and in Tunis itself no less than 4,000 persons occupy themselves with the manufacture of silk.

Perfumes. The most aristocratic form of commerce in Tunis is to keep one of the shops in the Suk Attarin (perfume bazaar). These are generally the property of wealthy Arabs of ancient lineage, who consider it good form to have something to do and accordingly spend a few hours there every day gossiping with their friends, and looking upon customers as a bore. There is a tradition that they are in many cases descended from the Moors of Spain, and that each of them still cherishes among his most valued possessions the key of the house which his ancestors once owned at Granada. The specialities in the way of perfumes are essences of violet and geranium, which cannot be procured elsewhere in such excellence. These and the usual essences of roses, orange blossom, jasmin, etc., are distilled as a home industry in primitive alembics all over the country, but more particularly at Sfax and Nabeul, which are surrounded by wonderful gardens.

Arms. The armourers' bazaar at Tunis is at first sight disappointing. There are none of the wonderful old weapons which are to be found in the

THE PERFUME BAZAAR.

Bezestin at Constantinople, and the supply of Damascus blades is neither better nor more genuine than in the average Oriental bazaar. But the modern arms to be found at Tunis possess a certain beauty and originality. There are long guns with octagonal barrels, beautifully chased in silver with inscriptions and fantastic designs; finely carved stocks; lumbering, but exceedingly decorative pistols; and swords or daggers with chased and jewelled hilts of characteristic native pattern. Moreover, the prices, after due haggling, are exceedingly moderate.

Potteries. Tunisian pottery is, perhaps, dying harder than almost any other industry. Its headquarters are at Jerba and Nabeul. At Jerba there are still over 150 potteries for the manufacture of jars of an ancient and graceful model, handed down from the days of Ali Baba. At Nabeul over an hundred establishments occupy themselves with the creation of every kind of household implement, by a process very little different from that which may be observed almost anywhere in Europe. In Tunis, also, there is a bed of clay, where the potters' bazaar has established itself and turns out a number of rough but pleasing shapes. The square tiles, which may still be seen in many of the principal palaces and offer so great a delight to the artistic eye, are no longer made, except on a very small scale and to order, as they have not been able to stand the competition of the cheap squares of cement which satisfy the modern taste.

Halfa-Grass. The cultivation of halfa-grass is, owing to its simplicity, one of the most popular industries in Tunis. At all periods of the year, throughout the greater part of the Regency, the natives eke out their livelihood by plucking this grass, which grows readily upon the most ungrateful soil. It may also be cut, but this involves the complete destruction of the plant. Large supplies are exported to England for making paper, and the remainder is either given to the cattle or used for weaving into rope, baskets and all manner of other useful objects. You will scarce find a native anywhere who does not know how to make something out of halfa-grass, which affords excellent opportunities for the utilization of every spare moment. Reed and palm leaves are also used largely in weaving, particularly for making mats, fly-whisks, fans, sun-hats, and all manner of baskets.

Trade with the Interior. From time immemorial, caravans have plied across the Sahara to effect an exchange between the best treasures of the savages of Central Africa and the worst products of European civilization. For many centuries, under the Arabs, the transit of the desert was fairly safe, easy, and regular, but since the establishment of the French in North Africa, it has become more and more difficult. As the Sahara presents a zone about a thousand miles wide, it can only be crossed by having recourse to watering-places at fixed points,—which are just as necessary as coaling stations to steamers at sea. In fact, the more you contemplate the desert, the more you are struck by its similarities to an ocean. It has ports, islands, storms, pirates, loneliness, and almost every other characteristic of the sea. There are, or have been until recently, seven recognised caravan lines, which are as important to be noticed and learned by heart by all students of Africa as the railways of Europe are by the modern strategist. Beginning at the West, the first two lines are from Timbuctoo to Morocco and Algiers. The third and fourth, starting from Kano (which is about half-way between the Niger and Lake Chad), proceed together as far as Asiu, whence the third (now almost entirely abandoned for fear of the Tuaregs) proceeds to Biskra, and the fourth (now about the only one in regular use) goes by way of Rhat and Rhadames to Tripoli. The fifth proceeds from Kuka, on Lake Chad, through Fezzan to Tripoli. The sixth is from Abesh to Benghazi. The seventh unites El-Fasher with Egypt. These caravan lines, which have existed, with small variation, since Carthaginian times, have been the main arteries for spreading Muhammadanism all over Africa—a fact which explains that the lines to Algeria and the attempt to divert the fourth line into Tunisia should have proved hopeless failures. As if the French had not already sufficient difficulties to cope with, they made the caravan lines, in which they were interested, still more impossible by attempting to set up custom houses at the ports of the desert.

Some statistics, necessarily dependent, to a great extent, upon guess-work, give the following as the value of the caravan trade during 1890: Line 1. £68,000; 2, £30,000; 4, £120,000; 5 and 6, £220,000. These are significant, as they show that Tripoli enjoys four-fifths of the whole caravan trade, Algeria and Tunisia none at all. The falling off of this caravan trade had been surprisingly rapid. At the middle of this century the trade across the Sahara represented between two and three millions sterling a year, and that was already a great falling off from preceding years. Now the whole trade is less than £440,000. The ambition of the French is, of course, to seize the whole trade of the Sahara by constructing a railway either from Biskra or Gabes to Lake Chad and the Niger; but any nation which could obtain permission from the Sultan to build a trans-Saharan railway, with a terminus either at Tripoli or Benghazi, would make a much better start. It would be like a literary man who preferred to invest in an already fairly flourishing newspaper, rather than to court disaster by starting a new one, or attempting to resuscitate one long since dead.

In the meanwhile, the French flatter themselves that they may be able to divert the fourth of the seven lines at Rhadames, so that instead of going to Tripoli it shall make its way to Gabes and Tunis. The possession of this line would serve the French as a very useful argument when questions of the partition of the Mediterranean hinterland came up. But, so far, all attempts to pacify the Tuaregs have proved unavailing, not because this people is quite so ferocious as baffled Frenchmen seek to make out, but because France has no idea of the right way to set about the work of conciliation.

Another absurd pretension on the part of the French is that all the hinterlands of the Mediterranean belong to the nations which own the coasts at the same longitude. On the strength of this they hint at a claim to the possession of Rhadames and Rhat, because they are west of the longitude of Zarzis, the frontier on the coast between Tunisia and Tripoli. It would not surprise me to hear at any moment that they had made a raid upon these towns. Rhadames and Rhat are, however, Tripolitan towns, occupied by Turkish garrisons and mentioned in treaties; and, whatever dispositions have been made for the distribution of hinterlands, they can only apply to those which had not previously received effective occupation. Between 1890 and 1896 some slow progress was made in the endeavours to set up a caravan trade between Rhadames and Tatawin, the southernmost Tunisian outpost. But the death of the Marquis de Morès at the hands of the Tuaregs produced strained relations which have never been healed up, and now the attempt has been virtually abandoned.

<small>Rhadames.</small> Rhadames is a little town of some 8,000 souls, with an oasis of less than 200 acres and 60,000 palm trees, which produce indifferent dates. The town has a more prosperous colony sixty miles to the East, at the oasis of Derj, where there are 450,000 palm trees. The Turkish garrison at Rhadames consists of 100 infantry and 20 cavalry. The chief goods to be found in the markets of Rhadames are—(1) European cotton goods, woollens, silks, glass, sugar, etc.; (2) Tunisian and Tripolitan woollen stuffs, made-up clothes, carpets, sheshias, and embroideries; (3) Soudanese ivory, ostrich feathers, wax, gums, silks,

scents, gold dust, and the tanned skins of buffaloes, antelopes, etc. As the caravans are, for the most part, loaded and unloaded at Rhadames, the merchants there, who make great profits as middle-men, would not by any means welcome the appearance of rival traders from Tunisia, or the passage towards the interior of caravans which had been made up elsewhere. They therefore constitute an important menace to the designs of the French.

Rhat. Some 360 miles south of Rhadames, in the centre of the Tuareg country, is Rhat, the most important market of the Sahara, if not of the world. A great fair is held there in the winter, and traders come thither from every quarter of the Sahara—from Timbuctoo, from Lake Chad, from Kano and the Niger, from Morocco, Tripoli, Benghazi, and the uttermost parts of Nubia and Lybia. It has some 5,000 inhabitants, and is surrounded by a pretty little oasis. The Turks have had a garrison of fifty foot soldiers there since 1854. In 1886 the Tuaregs massacred this garrison; but it was replaced by another in the following year, when an arrangement was arrived at between the Tuaregs and the Turks.

The Tuaregs. Some 20,000 Tuaregs occupy, nomadically but effectually, a country as large as France. They have a reputation for courage and fierce intractability. Between their tribes they are said to act generously and even chivalrously, but with strangers there is no cruelty or treachery too bad for them. There is a long list of travellers who have succumbed to them during the last thirty years, and the only way of passing through their country in safety, is to proceed with a large and well-armed escort, turning neither to the right hand nor to the left and mistrusting every proposal which may come from them. They exact a tribute from every one who passes, and, if it were possible to trust them, this tribute would be well earned as the price of protection. But their character is such that all who have had anything to do with them despair of ever being able to repose the least confidence in them. This is probably their best safeguard, and they wisely realize that any terms with France would inevitably lead to their subjection. The French are never tired of scheming to accomplish this last and most necessary preliminary to their establishment of a caravan line; but I am convinced that this line is only one more of the many mirages which are called up by too long a contemplation of the ever fascinating desert.

<small>Agricultural Methods.</small> Most colonists, except the very poorest, come to Tunisia with the intention of investing in land and employing the natives to work it for their benefit. The methods in vogue are either (1) to hire labourers and superintend them personally, or (2) to let out the land to natives in return for the greater part of the profits. Local use specifies five elements for the cultivation of land: capital, cattle, agricultural implements, labour, and the land itself. The purchaser, therefore, providing four out of the five requirements, stipulates for four-fifths of the proceeds, and natives are easily induced to accept

these oppressive terms, giving their whole labour and rarely contriving to earn more than £5 a year. Day labourers, when they are employed, are paid from 8d. to 1s. a day, or, at harvest time, from 10d. to 1s. 6d. Others are hired at 24s. the month, or from £5 to £10 the year; those who engage for less than a year having no certitude of regular employment. Those who accept the *khammes*, or fifth of the returns, often sell themselves into something scarcely distinguishable from slavery. The colonist gives them a certain sum down and they must give him all their time and labour until the debt shall have been wiped off. Another system, known as *mrharsa*, is sometimes accepted. By this the colonist provides the land, and the labourer engages himself to plant and tend olives, fig-trees, orange-trees, cactus, or whatever other plants the colonist may select, in view of a partition on ungenerous lines. Things, however, often right themselves through the fact that the labourer is compelled to demand further advances before he can complete his engagement.

Agricultural methods are still very primitive in Tunisia. In the more prosperous parts a horse or a camel is used for ploughing, but elsewhere it is not unusual to find an unfortunate woman harnessed to it in company with a milch cow or even a donkey.

Tunisia comprises some 30,000,000 acres and a population of 1,800,000 inhabitants. About 5,000,000 acres are still unappropriated. Of those which are appropriated, a large proportion are held in common by the tribes of the south, and most of the remainder are owned in common by families which have not exercised the right of subdivision. 1,250,000 acres are state domains, a large proportion of which have not been cultivated at all.

Habbus. The most noteworthy form of land tenure is that known as the *habbu*, a kind of mortmain, which at one time embraced fully a quarter of the soil of Tunisia. Originally *habbus* were constituted only for religious or philanthropic purposes, but later on there was no necessity for them to have any reference to a pious work. In that case they were known as private *habbus*, the document of incorporation enumerating the person or persons benefitting by them, and the property only reverting to beneficent objects on the failure of all male issue. In any case the *habbus* were for ever inalienable, but this caused such grave inconveniences that the Beys were forced to decree that they might be exchanged for other land, or might even be let for long leases so long as there was no actual sale. These leases are known as *enzels*, and the owner of them is held to pay every year a sum of money to the owner of the *habbu*. He is not a tenant, for his title is perpetual; he is not an owner, for the *habbus* are inalienable. Many colonists, who have secured *habbu* land, hope that some day the Government may be induced to turn their fixed tenure into freeholds.

Wells. The supply of water is naturally one of the chief considerations in Africa, and special effort is directed towards the creation of wells. They are generally very deep and may be observed in every part of the country, surmounted by scaffolding and masonry. There is a kind of pulley with skin buckets at one end, and a horse or camel at the other. The animal is driven along a pathway until the full buckets issue from the mouth of the well, when he is driven back to recommence the operation. At most of the wells, particularly at periods when extensive irrigation is necessary, this process may be observed from early morning until past sunset.

Cactus. Huge hedges of cactus are one of the most familiar features of the landscape of Tunisia. The fruit, which is as tasteless and refreshing as the water melon, is largely consumed during the hot weather, and the green rackets are, in spite of their prickles, very popular fodder with all kinds of cattle. An acre of ground will produce 20,000 lbs. of fruit, or from 25,000 to 30,000 lbs. of fodder,—one or the other, for if the rackets are sacrificed there will be no Barbary figs. But the growth of rackets for fodder is considered the more profitable.

Vines. Great efforts are being made in the interests of viticulture in Tunisia, but so far the wine is so exceedingly nasty that it is scarcely of any value, even for adulterating the claret of the English middle classes. Phylloxera has not yet made its appearance in Tunisia—a great proof of the good taste of the microbe—and at one time there were very sanguine hopes for the prospects of Tunisian wine-making; but, just as everything seemed to have been put into order, the French vineyards began to recover from their maladies and those of Tunisia had perforce to return to their obscurity. The heavy fall in the price of wine (20s. to 10s. and even 8s. per 22 gallons) four or five years ago made it almost impossible to produce wine in Tunisia at a profit; but since then there have been ups and downs in the trade, and it has been thought worth while to persevere. One reason why better success has not been obtained is that the Tunisian vine is much larger than the French, and accordingly requires different treatment, which the French workmen have obstinately refused to give it. There is also some difficulty in the manufacture of wine in Tunisia owing to the difficulty of reducing the temperature during fermentation. For this special and costly apparatus is required, and the local wine-makers have put off the expenditure as long as they could.

Olives. The presence of olive-trees in Tunisia has been noted ever since the days of the Romans, and the latest census gives no less than 12,000,000 trees, the tax upon which constitutes a large proportion of the national revenue. Some 2,300,000 trees are *habbu* property, in many cases endlessly subdivided. A French friend told me that he had recently bought the 35th part of a tree on *enzel* for a very few francs, more as a joke than anything else, in order to acquire an interest in the agricultural destinies of the country. There are some twenty different kinds of olives in the Regency, the oil they give becoming better and better as they come further south. The improved procedure introduced by the French in oil-making has nearly doubled the price of Tunisian oils. The planting of olive-trees is not, however, to be recommended to colonists desirous of obtaining a quick return for their investment, as an olive-tree only begins to bear fruit when it is ten years old and does not reach maturity until it is twenty. A long time must elapse before the oil production of Tunisia can have a serious effect upon the European market. At present the annual production of France is 300,000 quintals of oil worth £1,720,000, that of Italy 1,300,000 quintals worth £7,800,000, that of Spain 3,000,000 quintals worth £11,600,000, while that of Tunisia is 200,000 quintals worth £600,000, a price which suffices to show how marked is the inferiority of the Tunisian oil.

Fisheries. The fishing industry has long been one of the foremost in Tunisia, and now affords employment to over 60,000 persons. The best fisheries have, however, been appropriated by French companies, and great care is taken that the natives shall enjoy little or none of the profits of their craft. All the fisheries are readily granted as concessions to any one whom the French Government may consider deserving of its favour. There is scarcly any control over the methods employed, which are accordingly of the most recklessly extravagant character, entirely without consideration for the future of the fisheries. These are so wealthy that such methods do not afford an immediate menace, but at the present rate there is little prospect of many fish surviving the present generation. The company which has appropriated the fishing rights in the

Lake of Bizerta catches several thousand pounds' weight every day, and exports the greater part of it direct to Marseilles. Two Frenchmen who hold the concession of fishing in the Lake of Tunis catch 3,000 pounds' weight a day. All along the Eastern coast of the Regency fishing is more or less abundant, and at Mahdia for forty days in May and June every year no less than 500,000 lbs. of a kind of sardine are caught and salted for exportation to Austria, Italy, and Greece. From Cape Kadija to Zarzis there is a stretch of coast which has no equal as a fishery in any other part of the world, and in the Kerkenna islands, opposite Sfax, practically the whole population is given up to fishing, and contrives to prosper in spite of the constant depredations of Italian and Greek poachers. The existence of a tide in the Gulf of Gabes is of particular assistance to the fishing.

While I was at Tunis I was constantly struck by the great superiority of the fish over that which is found on the other side of the Mediterranean. As a rule they were precisely the same kind but of infinitely better quality. There was a John Dory which, when perfectly fresh, was as different from the John Dory we know in England as gold from dross.

<small>Sponges.</small> Three kinds of sponges are found off Tunisia, varying in price from a shilling to a sovereign, and are taken in three different ways. The Arabs and Sicilians use a kind of trident at the end of a pole, sometimes as much as fifteen yards long. If there be the slightest ripple, it is impossible to see

through the water. Until twenty years ago these fishermen secured the necessary calmness by pouring a few drops of oil on the surface of the water; but this was an extravagant plan, and now they generally use a tin cylinder, some twelve by twenty-four inches, provided at the end with a piece of glass. By dipping this below the surface of the water, it is possible to see the bottom as clearly as if the surface were perfectly calm. Having made out where the best sponges are, a fisherman halts his boat and plunges his trident straight down, when a slight twist suffices to uproot and secure a sponge. The Greeks use a *gangava*, or drag, which is a kind of frame with a net in the middle. Three sides of it are of wood and the other is a strong iron bar. It is attached to a rope and dragged along the bottom of the sea by the motion of the boat, tearing up the sponges and collecting them in the net. As soon as it is full, the boat becomes difficult to propel, the net is brought up, and its contents, consisting of sponges, all manner of shells, and even large fish, are taken out and sorted before the drag is let down again. This is a very extravagant and destructive method of fishing, for it roots up a great many sponges which it does not collect. The Turkish Government has long forbidden it at Tripoli, but in Tunisian waters it is only restricted by a close season in March, April and May. The natives of Jerba and the Kerkenna islands prefer the more sporting method of diving. This only takes place at a depth of twelve or fifteen feet, and each diver is provided with a knife, to defend himself against sharks, and with a net at his waist to carry the sponges. 1000 natives, 700 Greeks and 800 Sicilians are engaged upon the sponge fisheries, and the Government takes care to collect a substantial revenue from their labours, over £4,000 a year being paid for the right to fish, besides a duty of nearly 2*d.* the lb. on every sponge exported.

Pulps. Some 65,000 lbs. of pulps are sold every year at Sfax alone, and their collection forms an important industry all along the coast. They are taken by divers, or by spearing, or in wicker-work traps. The pulp is an evil-looking and evil-tasting mollusc, which is largely consumed in Greece, particularly during Lent. When it has been caught, a hard membrane is removed from its head, which is then beaten with several hundreds of blows, to complete the killing of the creature and render its flesh somewhat less like a brick-bat. Then any remains of sea-water are squeezed out and it is hung up to dry in the sun.

Chapter IX

JUSTICE AND EDUCATION

Justice—The Court of the Kadi—The Governor of Tunis—Public Executions—Prisons—The Right of Sanctuary—Capital Punishment—The Paradise of Criminals—Police Precautions—Modern Solomons—Education—Sadiki College—Alawi College.

Justice. In each district of Tunisia the administration of justice is entrusted to Kadis for civil and Kaïds for criminal matters. Justice is still nominally free, but practically very expensive owing to the corruption of the officials. The Koran is the civil and criminal code of the natives. In theory the Bey is the supreme court of appeal, but he has delegated this function to two tribunals, known as the Uzara and the Sharaa. The Uzara is concerned with everything excepting real property and probate. All its decisions require ratification by the Bey, who goes through them with some care. For personal injuries there is a regular tariff of blood money like the Germanic *Wehrgeld*, but in the case of murder the relatives cannot be compelled to accept it. The Sharaa is a religious tribunal for appeals from the judgments of the Kadis on matters outside the province of the Uzara.

Besides the native tribunals there are also French

courts, to which all Europeans are amenable now that the capitulations, which gave them the benefit of their own consular courts, have been weakly abandoned. There are at present two tribunals of first instance and ten magistrates' courts in the principal localities; in five others the contrôleur civil exercises judicial authority. The French themselves admit that the legal procedure they have introduced into Tunisia is far too costly and cumbersome for the needs of the place, and there are many complaints that there is no French court of appeal.

The Court of the Kadi There are few things so delightfully old fashioned and picturesque as a Muhammadan court of justice. I entered a large hall, painted black and white, with pillars striped liked zebras. A crowd of men, Europeans and Jews as well as Arabs, were lounging about in the centre. Four draped recesses, suggesting "cosy corners" or the shrines of a temple, were railed off and guarded by native policemen. In each recess was a long divan, where a Kadi sat in gorgeous robes with his legs tucked away under him and only a bit of bright yellow slipper peeping out. In front of him was a long wooden bench where the litigants sat facing him. Most of them were Arabs, but occasionally a Jew or an European plaintiff was among them. The Kadi wore a very grave but very benevolent expression. In his hand was a string of beads, which he fingered very slowly with a slight clicking sound. Otherwise he remained motionless for the greater part of the time, excepting when he raised his hands aloft as a sign of astonishment or displeasure. He listened very patiently to what each party had to say and himself spoke very little, asking only a few questions, and then pronouncing a summary judgment. Each case took three minutes or less to dispose of. Once I caught his eye fixed upon me with a very severe expression, so I went off to the other side and watched another Kadi, a musty old man with a green turban. His procedure seemed almost identical, except that he raised his hands much oftener, somehow reminding me of a marionette. The Kadis on one side of the hall give judgment according to the Malekite rite, those on the other side according to the Hanefite. As one is much stricter than the other it is not infrequent for a defendant, who is dissatisfied with a judgment according to one rite, to go across the hall and have his case tried over again according to the other rite. When I came outside, I saw a fine white mule tied to the door-way, richly caparisoned with gold and silver embroidery, and was told that it was waiting there for the Kadi.

The Governor of Tunis. After visiting the native courts of justice, Mrs. Vivian and I strolled in with our guide to the palace where the Governor of Tunis directs the administration of the native police. I thought we were merely going to be shown something more of the machinery of native justice, and I was somewhat taken aback when I found that we were being conducted straight into the Governor's private room. "These are the chambers of the various police inspectors," said the guide, "and this is the

Governor." I could not help thinking of the story
of the undergraduate who took a party of ladies
across a college court and, after pointing to a window
and saying, "Those are the Dean's rooms," threw up a
pebble, adding, as an angry face peered out, "and that
is the Dean." However, the Governor seemed to
take it quite as a matter of course, and I learned afterwards that all tourists who go the round of the palace
are taken in for a chat and a cup of coffee with him.
He made us very welcome, and, seating us beside him
on a divan, proceeded to converse, the guide acting
as interpreter. After the usual compliments about
the intense pleasure it gave him to receive us, he
inquired how we liked Tunis. "Tell him," said Mrs.
Vivian, "that I find it very interesting." The guide,
who combined the stupidity and mischief of his class to
an extraordinary degree, promptly told the Governor
that she found him very interesting. We could not
make out at first why he seemed so much taken aback
by a commonplace remark, but when he replied "Old
men are always interesting," we could only say that
we should never have imagined that he was old.

<small>Public Executions.</small> I had been looking forward to attending
a public execution one morning, but the
disappointing information of a reprieve came in at
the last moment. Formerly the public were allowed
to throng round the very steps of the scaffold, and
the photographers of the town sell gruesome pictures
of all details; but now there is a military cordon, and
only specially favoured spectators are admitted within
it. More interesting than the execution itself are the

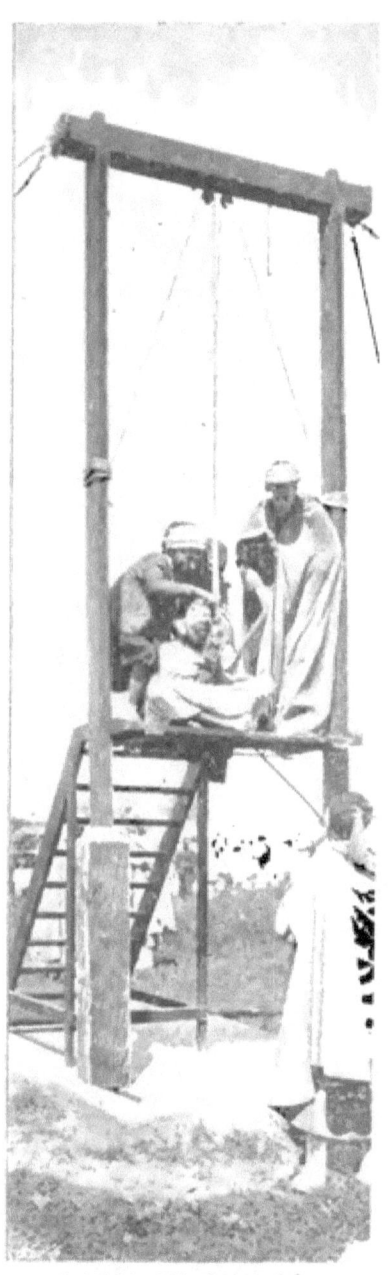

A PUBLIC EXECUTION (I).

preliminaries, which take place in the hall of justice at the Bardo Palace. The Bey seats himself on his great gilt throne upholstered with red velvet, and the murderer is brought before him to be confronted with his victim's family. The Bey then inquires of the victim's family if they are willing to accept the blood-money. It is a sum of about £29, to be paid by the murderer; but if, as is generally the case, he does not possess so much money, the Bey makes it up out of his private purse. It is, however, unusual for the money to be accepted, and the family which thus forwent vengeance would expose itself to considerable contumely. But the Bey, like the Sultan and the Emperor

A PUBLIC EXECUTION (2).

of Austria, has a great aversion from taking life, even in the case of murderers, and he always does his best to persuade the family to accept. If they remain obdurate, he turns his back and pretends not to know what is about to happen. The murderer is then taken out and hanged. The Bey is now a very old man, and he shrinks more and more from the necessity of coming to the Bardo from his palace at Marsa, some twelve miles away, for these functions. So pressure is always brought to bear on the victim's family some days before the time fixed for the execution. When blood-money is accepted, the murderer is sent to penal servitude for life. The Moslem penal code is based on

the Mosaic dispensation. Does a man gouge out another's eye, cut off his hand, or take his life, he must, unless pecuniary compensation be accepted, pay for his crime with eye, hand, or life.

Had I stayed in Tunis a few days longer, I should have had an opportunity of witnessing a triple execution. The victims were three out of a band of four Arabs, who committed murder and highway robbery near Tozeur in August, 1897. The fourth man was killed at the time of the crime, and these three were condemned on the 11th of April, 1898. In the case of a premeditated crime like this, blood-money is not admitted, so the presence of the Bey was a mere formality. He arrived at the Bardo by special train at 8.20 a.m., and proceeded at once to the throne room, where, after the various high functionaries of the court had gone through the ceremony of kissing hands, the three criminals were brought before him. According to usage the three men made a formal appeal for mercy, though they knew full well that there was no hope. The Bey looked at them sadly, but it was with a firm voice that he exclaimed, for all answer, "Turn them toward the gate of the Bardo," which is the local euphemism for "Let the law take its course." The men were then conducted to a room in the basement, where their eyes were bandaged and their hands fastened with iron padlocks, after which they were led out to be hanged in the open. The youngest of the culprits, who was only twenty-five years of age, seemed inert with fear, and his execution took no less than eleven minutes to effect. But the other two, aged twenty-six and thirty-five respectively, displayed all the courage begotten of Moslem fatalist doctrines. In accordance with a new regulation, the crowd was kept off by a military cordon; but there were many officials, pressmen, and privileged spectators in the immediate neighbourhood of the scaffold.

Prisons. One of my first requests from the Residency was for permission to visit the prisons. I was told, with a great show of courtesy, that I might see anything I chose, but each time that I recalled my wish to see the prisons I was put off. I persevered for nearly three months, but was always met with some ingenious excuse. This served to strengthen my belief in the statement, which was made to me by several disinterested residents, that the prisons are in a disgraceful condition.

The Right of Sanctuary. As I have pointed out, native murderers cannot be reprieved by the Bey, and their sentences can only be commuted if the victims' families accept blood-money. It is still possible, however, to secure absolute immunity from punishment for any crime by the simple expedient of taking refuge in a sanctuary. In old days the sanctuaries were very numerous, and included not only certain mosques, but also several shrines, cemeteries, Koranic schools, quarters of Tunis, and villages. The number of these has now been largely reduced, but there are still many places where the

Bey's writ does not run. A few years ago, one of the sights of Tunis was a refugee, who occupied a meadow in sanctuary just off a boulevard near the Kasbah. He had been there sixteen years, his friends brought him the necessaries of life, and his solitude was shared by a cow. Though he had murdered a man, no one attempted to violate his sanctuary. But the family of his victim had neither forgiven nor forgotten. The dead man's sons kept constant guard, day and night, near the entrance to the sanctuary, lest perchance the murderer, lulled by a false sense of security, should one day venture forth. Their sons, too, as they grew up, took their turns at a watch, which they were taught to consider a sacred trust. Surely, among no other people might we look for so patient and relentless a vengeance, thus handed down to the third generation. At last, after sixteen years of ceaseless vigilance on both sides, the watchers were rewarded. The refugee's cow broke her tether one evening, and wandered out of the sanctuary. Her owner peered out after her and saw no one about—no one whom he could ask to bring her back and no one whom he need fear. The cow was strolling down the empty road, and her loss would have been a serious one to him. He determined to run the risk. But no sooner had he gone ten yards outside than his enemies sprang out from their ambush, triumphantly secured him, and carried him off to prison. The affair created an immense sensation. In view of the long period which had elapsed since the crime, unheard-of efforts were made on the criminal's behalf. The Bey, the Muftis, the Sheikh-ul-Islam, and many other prominent Moslems interceded with the victim's family to induce them to accept the blood-money, but they were obdurate, and there was nothing for it but to allow the law to take its course. The whole family gathered round the scaffold, even the sick rising from their beds or being carried in litters, to witness the act of reparation, without which they felt they had been dishonoured.

Capital Punishment. It is strange how deep-rooted is the sympathy between modern Italians and crime. Not content with abolishing capital punishment in their peninsula, they spare no efforts to save their murderers abroad. It was natural that they should make special efforts in Tunisia, where they fancy they have lingering claims to share in the Government. At the time of the late treaty, they succeeded in extorting a protocol, which, however, guarantees little. The French undertake therein that no Italian subject shall be put to death without a special reference to the President of their Republic, who will take into consideration the state of the law in Italy. This protocol was understood to be more or less secret, but as it has now been published in a Yellow Book, there can be no harm in referring to it. Nothing definite is promised, but the evident intention is that Italian murderers shall, if possible, be reprieved. A case in point arose not long ago, when an Italian was condemned to death for a murder of particular brutality. The *Unione*, the Italian daily paper at

Tunis, though usually correct in its attitude, protested vehemently against the condemnation and cited the protocol. This was exceedingly indiscreet, for it seemed to set up a claim that there should be one law for Italians and another, less generous, for Frenchmen in the Regency. If anything was likely to turn the scale against a reprieve, it was this kind of contention, and though the man's life was spared, he had no cause to thank the zeal of his compatriots.

The Paradise of Criminals. I may cite another case in illustration of the temper of Italian justice. An Italian, recently arrested in Tunis, was found to have been sentenced, twelve months previously, to a term of twenty years' imprisonment for murder. At first it was thought that he must have escaped, as many do, from the Italian penal colony at Pantellaria hard by. But it was found on inquiry that he had been released at the end of six months, as a reward for good conduct in prison, with the sole condition that he should never set foot on Italian soil again. Though evidence of tenderness to criminals, this can scarcely be commended as a neighbourly act.

Police Precautions. Emigration is so often the last refuge of the scoundrel that colonies require special safeguards for controlling the exotic population. So far the Government of Tunis has found the presence of undesirable Europeans a constant anxiety, and special precautions have now been taken. In future, every settler (temporary tourists, of course, excepted) must produce his *casier judiciaire*. This and the *carnet militaire* are documents which answer in Latin countries to the Russian passport, and I understand that any Frenchman, who loses his *carnet militaire*, is liable to punishment equally with a passportless Russian. The *casier judiciaire* is a document which any Frenchman may obtain at any time from the mayor of his birthplace, to whom all judicial condemnations are notified. It specifies the absence of condemnations or the number of condemnations which an individual has undergone, and must be produced on important occasions. The system is useful, but troublesome and by no means infallible. A friend of mine, who was recently applying for a post at Saint Cyr, sent for his *casier judiciaire*, and found to his amazement that he was registered as having undergone a whole series of condemnations. He took it to the authorities and protested that he had never come into conflict with the law. "Not only have you been frequently sentenced," was the astounding reply, "but you are at this present moment undergoing a sentence of six months' imprisonment for theft!" It turned out that my friend had had his papers stolen and used by a professional criminal. Had the criminal not chanced to be actually in prison at the time that the papers were called for, it would have been well nigh impossible to rectify the error, and my friend's whole career might have been shattered. As it was, there were endless formalities and difficulties before the matter could be set right, and a special decree had to be promulgated in his favour. The present proposal is to call for the *casiers judiciaires* of the citizens of countries where the system is in force, and individuals with infamous antecedents will be invited to leave the Regency at once. Citizens of other countries, such as Great Britain, may be called on to prove their respectability by some other means.

<small>Modern Solomons.</small> A recent French judgment may be cited as an illustration of Arab matters and Gallic astuteness. An Arab was travelling through the interior with his wife: he was on donkey-back, and she was afoot. By came a rich Arab on horseback and offered her a lift behind him. She accepted, and presently, in the course of the journey, confided that she was unhappily married. Her companion proposed a plan by which she might elope with him, and she agreed to it readily. Accordingly, when they came to a branch road, they increased their pace and paid no heed to the protestations of the husband, who was soon left behind. He succeeded in tracking them to the horseman's village, only to find that precautions had been taken against his arrival; for everybody asserted that they had known the runaway pair for many years as husband and wife, and that the real husband must be an impudent impostor. The unfortunate man had recourse to the French, who were at first puzzled how to act in the face of a village's unanimous testimony. At last a happy thought occurred to the judge. He placed the real husband's dogs in one room, those of the other man in another, and confronted the

woman with both. Arab dogs are very faithful to their own households and very fierce towards all strangers; so, though she did her utmost to irritate her own dogs, they could not be restrained from fawning on her, and though she lavished every blandishment toward the dogs of her new home, they barked and showed their teeth with ever-increasing fury. The judge thereupon ordered her to be given back to her real husband, and he placarded the village with the following notice: "The testimony of one dog is here more to be believed than that of ten Arabs." As the title of dog is one of the Arabs' worst terms of opprobrium, this notice was deemed a worse punishment than fines or imprisonment. I commend this idyll to any novelist who may be in search of a plot.

Education.   Schools with the Moslems are merely an adjunct to the mosque, and the teaching is nearly all of a religious character. This the French have not yet ventured to interfere with, but they have set up schools of their own with the intention of undermining the national sentiment, and have endeavoured, in the case of the higher educational establishments of the natives, by seizing the control of the finances, to obtain possession of the active side of the establishment.

The two principal establishments at Tunis are the Alawi and Sadiki colleges. The Alawi is a normal school for training teachers, and the Sadiki a superior primary school for Arabs. Before the occupation, every attempt at education, except the Sadiki college, was more or less of a Christian missionary character, and, as such, was viewed with suspicion by the natives. The establishment started at Carthage in 1880, under the name of the S. Louis College, by Cardinal Lavigerie, was transferred in the following year to Tunis, under the name of S. Charles's College.

In 1896 there were 109 French scholastic establishments in Tunisia, attended by 15,088 boys and girls,

A MOSLEM SCHOOL.

including 2,455 French, 2,457 Italians, 1,572 Maltese, 4,143 Moslems (of whom 21 were girls), and 4,055 Jews. The subjects taught in the schools under the control of the French Government are the three R's, geography (particularly that of the Mediterranean), the history of France and North Africa, the French language, science, drawing, music, gymnastics for the boys, and sewing for the girls. The method employed is the same as in France, but the buildings still leave much to be desired. The establishment to which the

French attach most importance is the Lycée Carnot, which is paid for by the Tunisians, and exists almost solely for the benefit of the French and the Jews. There is also a secondary school for girls, the chief object of which is to provide teachers for the girls' schools throughout the Regency.

<small>Sadiki College.</small> The point about the Sadiki College is that the pupils are exclusively Moslems, and the attempt to imbue them with French notions is craftily veiled, so as not to alarm their susceptibilities. It was founded in 1876 by the Bey Sadiki, and endowed with a fortune confiscated from a disgraced minister. Since the French occupation it has been governed by a council of eight Frenchmen, according to the methods in vogue at German universities. There are fifty boarders and an hundred day pupils, none of whom pay anything towards their education. The programme of work suffices to show the scope of the institution as it is at present managed: (1) The French language, (2) French history and geography, (3) general history and geography, (4) arithmetic, according to the metric system, (5) mathematics, (6) drawing, and (7) physical science. Successful pupils generally find their way into the Government service of the Protectorate.

I found the director an agreeable man, but rotten to the core with European prejudices. From the beginning to the end of my visit he never ceased to expatiate upon the benefits of new-fangled arrangements, and he was perfectly convinced that the introduction of washhand-stands in the place of a tap, and marble-topped tables instead of a kind of trough in the dining-hall, were civilizing influences of incalculable benefit. After showing me over the whole establishment and drawing my special attention to the scientific laboratories, he told me that he relied chiefly upon them for the perfection of the civilizing work on which he was engaged.

"You can have no idea," he said, "until you have tried, what an up-hill business it is. The Arabs seem to have inside their heads"—and he tapped his forehead significantly—"a kind of clod which renders them impervious to modern ideas. We may contrive to disturb it a little, so that one or two sensible notions may filter in, but to attempt to dislodge it is hopeless — at any rate in our time. We can but lay the foundations of a work which will take generations to conclude. It is disheartening enough, and at times I am tempted to despair; but then I reflect that civilization, however slow in its operation, is irresistible, and that what I am doing now may some day bring forth fruit, the extent of which it is impossible for us to conceive. Picture to yourself," he went on, "the average Arab believes, and has been taught from time immemorial, that the earth is a flat sheet, supported by an elephant, which is supported by a camel, which in its turn is supported by a whole series of fabulous animals. You may prove to him that the earth is round and travels through space round the sun, and he will listen very patiently to all you have to say; but he begins by mistrusting you, and he goes away with precisely the same opinions which he had imbibed with his mother's milk. You see that it is all a matter of religion with him, and he always suspects you of a covert intention to wean him from his ancient faith. I am far from denying that he possesses many excellent qualities and some high capabilities. But these are so distorted that they are rather an obstacle than a help to his advancement. For instance, there is scarcely one amongst my pupils who is not a wonderful draughtsman. He will produce the most accurate drawings and then spoil everything by giving way to some freak of his fanciful imagination. This is particularly the case when we allow him the use of the colour-box, and he takes an inexpressible delight in the creation of strange monstrosities, such as a blue horse or a scarlet elephant or a man with seven heads. It is all exquisite in its way, and he is unrivalled as a decorator, for all his conceptions are harmonious; but he is not practical, and, most discouraging of all, you can never hope to make him see why or where he is wrong. At present the only result of all our attempts at education is that those who seem to take most kindly to it and profit by it most, turn out the worst rascals and the most fanatical in their adherence to their old habits and customs."

"Then why not leave them alone?" I asked innocently.

He looked aghast for a moment, and then replied that, though he admitted the present results were discouraging, the blessings of civilization must undoubtedly make themselves felt in the long run.

"Rash man!" I exclaimed; "you little know what you are doing. Here is a noble race which has thriven for centuries on ideas which you are incapable of understanding. You may succeed in destroying what you term the 'clod' in the Arab's mind, but before you are able to put anything in to replace it, you will let loose upon the world a conscienceless monster, who will not be responsible for his actions and may drift into incalculable mischief. You are seeking to do on a large scale what the mad scoundrels of your own revolution accomplished in a smaller sphere last century, and it will serve your nation right if she be swept away in the cataclysm which will ensue."

In old times this college possessed vast *habbu* properties, but a grasping minister of the Bey arranged for their concession on *enzel* at a nominal rent in perpetuity, and even transferred the *enzel* in some cases as a charge upon some tumble-down shanty in the native quarter. The natural result was that the *enzel*, being higher than the fair rent of the shanty, soon remained unpaid, and the property of the college degenerated woefully. What now remains has only been rescued by a spoiling of the spoiler on even more high-handed lines.

In one of the rooms I was introduced to a number of Arab notaries, who are still permitted to control a portion of the business side of the administration of the college. As education among the Moslems is considered a branch of religion, these notaries were all ecclesiastical dignitaries. I was struck by the contrast between their effusive welcome and the off-hand manner of most of the French officials in the college, but of course I was not permitted to do more than exchange the usual salutations with them. I understand, however, that their share in the work has now been reduced more or less to a farce, as is the case with the remains of Arab administration in all the other departments of the state. I noticed that their room had a separate entrance, so that they and those with whom they had business, might pass in without entering the college itself.

One of the few relics of the old establishment was a strange box in one of the class-rooms, which had evidently been preserved merely as a curiosity. It was a clumsy but very elaborate apparatus for exhibiting the effect of an electric current in a vacuum. It must have cost an immense amount of money and have been of exceedingly little use except as a toy. It consisted for the most part of tubes twisted into the shape of Arabic words, most of which had some reference to the donor, and there was an ingenious brass tongue, close to the floor, which released the electric current on being surreptitiously pressed by the foot. It would no doubt have been extremely useful for exhibition to a savage tribe, as a proof of the possession of magical powers.

Alawi College. The Alawi College is open to all races and creeds. Its special object is the production of teachers, and Frenchmen who come over to teach in the Regency generally begin with a short course of study here. Particular attention is paid to manual industries.

Mussulman schools concern themselves merely with teaching to read and write the Koran, which no teacher is permitted to try to interpret to his pupils. At the Mosque of the Olive at Tunis is the chief Muhammadan school, which recalls in many ways the mediæval universities, where theology was the principal subject. It is administered by the Sheikh-ul-Islam, and has 111 teachers. The pupils reside in special establishments, of which there are at Tunis 22, containing 450 rooms. Attached to this university is a chair of the Arabic language for the benefit of Europeans.

Chapter X

BEASTS AND FEATHERED FOWL

Camels — Locusts — Dogs — Flamingoes — Serpents — Scorpions — Gazelles.

I do not propose to attempt an exhaustive survey of the fauna of Tunisia, but a few notes on those creatures which I have observed may not be without interest.

Camels. It is by no means easy to obtain trustworthy information about camels in Africa, for it is everybody's pastime to invent extravagant stories about them, just as in America about snakes, or with us about dogs and cats. For instance, a lady, who travelled in Tunis some years ago, was told that young camels were habitually buried in the sand up to their eyes in order to straighten their necks. This she readily believed and solemnly inserted in her inevitable book as a piece of news.

In England we have a certain reverence for the camel. We stare at him in the Zoo with as much wonder as if he were a giraffe, and we remember our rides on the strange beast's back when we were short-coated. It is, therefore, rather a shock, on landing in

North Africa, to find camels lounging about the streets by the score, and to learn that they are rather cheaper than horses; £4 to £7 will purchase a very fair camel, which can easily carry a burthen of 660 lbs. for thirty miles a day during any number of days. An Arab does not think nearly as much of his camel as he does of his horse, nor even of his mule. It is only for the camel's strength and endurance that he is in such demand. These are the qualities which have earned him the name of the " ship of the desert." As everybody knows he can lay in a store of water in his pouch sufficient to last him many days. There is scarcely any food too tough and unpalatable for his digestion. Indeed, he has become notorious for his habit of feeding on the cactus or prickly pear. He does not choose this food, any more than the ass chooses thistles, as a delicacy ; but people talk of the cactus as camel's food just as we do of thistles for asses. A camel's ordinary food, however, consists of bran with the refuse of olives out of which the oil has been extracted. This is spread out for him in a mat. Directly he sees his dinner being brought, he exhibits great excitement, emitting a strange, soft, nasal sound, something between a growl and a very loud purr. He kneels down very deliberately, bringing down the fore-legs first and afterwards the hind-legs, and burrows his nose into the mat. A camel is never in a hurry, even for his meals, and each mouthful is chewed over and over again, even though goats and kids and fowls may all be poaching on the provision. When specially hard work is

THE CAMEL.

required, a camel is given a ration of barley and date-stones.

During my stay at Tunis, I found it a constant pleasure to wander into the *fonduks*, or camel-yards, and watch the animals at home there. Most of those I saw had been employed in carrying coals and were taking it easy until they should be needed again. Sometimes there would be only half a dozen, sometimes several hundreds in a yard. Those who had a tendency to wander had one of their fore-legs bent right back at the knee and securely tied, so that they could only hobble uncomfortably on three legs. This made them look very grotesque and ungainly, but did not actually hurt them. At halting-places on the march they are always tied up in this way.

Camels are said to be the most docile animals imaginable. It is true that, when they are walking the streets, they shrink from contact with any one and will swerve aside if they meet even a small child or a puppy. But this is entirely on their own account, for they have a dread of being touched, except by their drivers. They do not even like to be stroked. As they stalk about with their noses high in air, and their big, astonished eyes looking round superciliously, they seem to say that they are ready to carry big burdens and go without food or drink, but that they will tolerate no familiarities. My first instinct whenever I see an animal is to go up and pat it, but I have had to give up the practice in the case of camels, as they always show their teeth and growl at me most menacingly. A polite camel-driver told me that this was only because the camels were accustomed to see none but white clothes. I gather, however, that they always resent being touched by any one. But it is only at one period of the year that they are actually vicious. Then the females may be known by a foam which gathers round the edges of their mouths. If they bite you, it is not with their teeth, but with their lips, which are exceedingly strong and produce a bruise such as is obtained by slamming a door upon the fingers. Camels generally go about wearing thick muzzles of dried esparto grass, which is used for all manner of basket-making in North Africa; but the muzzles are merely to prevent their nibbling the branches of trees by the way. When they attack people, they generally trample upon them, and the effect of a hard battering with their soft feet is not unlike a tremendous pummelling with boxing gloves. Such violence is, however, quite the exception. As a rule, the camel is obedient, but not intelligent. He soon learns that a tap on his knees is an order to kneel or rise, and he is very accommodating when you want to mount or dismount. But he cannot for an instant be compared to a horse or a dog for his powers of thought. Camels never combine among themselves for any purpose whatever; they do not increase their pace in the very least when they are on their way back to their stable; and they have never been known to sham lameness in order to shirk work. On the other hand, they are models of obstinacy. No power on earth will induce a camel to do anything he considers unfair.

CAMELS DRAWING WATER FROM A WELL.

The proverb about the last straw is no fiction. Place a burthen, which is in the least degree too heavy, upon a camel's back, and wild horses will not persuade him to get up, let alone start upon his journey. And he must be left to fix its own pace. A whip, even across his nose, would have no effect whatever, and your spur might tear his flanks to pieces without increasing the pace a jot. If his rider irritate him, he will not try to kick him off, but may run away. If he does run away, he will take good care that you do not benefit by the momentary increase of speed. He will give you clearly to understand that he only sought to annoy you, and will never run away very far. His motion, when he runs away, is exceedingly disagreeable, and you soon agree that he has been well named the "ship of the desert" for more reasons than one. If you are not actually sea-sick, at any rate you feel very uncomfortable. Animals are notoriously more susceptible to sea-sickness than we are, and a friend of mine, who imported a number of zoological specimens from the interior of Africa on camel-back, found that most of them perished from the effect of the voyage.

Sometimes there are scenes of jealousy between male camels, and they fight with great fury. Once they have commenced to fight, it is impossible to separate them until one has killed the other. A camel which has been the victor in such a fight becomes very useful in guarding the flock of females. He wards off intruders, prevents the flock from wandering and brings it home safely at the end of the day, so that no keepers are necessary.

The pack-camel travels very slowly, and, until you are sufficiently reconciled to the motion to be able to doze on its back, you are constantly tempted to get off and walk. If you want speed, you must buy a racing camel. This seems to belong to a different creation. It is much taller, more alert, and more intelligent. It can accomplish 150 miles in sixteen hours without undue effort, and, in the matter of price, compares with the pack-camel as the thoroughbred does with the cab-horse. The racing camel is very carefully bred, and valuable prizes are offered by a racing society at Biskra for the fleetest racer. I have seen the start, and it reminded me, in a far-off sort of way, of Newmarket. The camels were all arranged in line, and they sniffed the air in their anxiety to be off. A flag was waved, and they set off at a terrible pace, as if they were only racing for a mile and a quarter. They kept together until they were almost out of sight. Then they seemed to settle down to their habitual pace, and the race proceeded with long intervals between the competitors. I have also seen the finish of a camel race, and it reminded me of the first motor-car promenade between London and Brighton. The camels were certainly not so broken down and bedraggled, but they came in at intervals of several hours, and great patience was necessary to watch them come in. It would be quite impossible to make a book on a camel race, for the pace of each camel is well known in advance, and the owners

CARAVAN PASSING THROUGH AN OASIS.

can make sure of winning or losing by several hours.

At the present day camels are used for all sorts of domestic purposes in Africa. They may even be seen drawing ploughs in the interior of the Regency of Tunis. You may remark a woman and a camel harnessed to the same plough, and you hesi-

A CAMEL TENT.

tate to decide which is the greater outrage. Camels are also used for drawing water from the strange, cumbersome, old-fashioned wells of North Africa. Their chief use, however, is for caravans. You may behold them bringing in huge cases of dates from the oases, or you may see them with great tent-like structures of red silk upon their backs. These tents are for the conveyance of Arab women of the upper classes, who seek to maintain the privacy of the harem even on a journey. Two women and some children are often accommodated on one camel. They have cushions on which they can lie down and even sleep. It is stuffy, and it is dark, but they deem themselves well off in escaping from the searching rays of the burning sun. And what an admirable disguise it affords! I am told that the authorities at Tripoli object to strangers travelling in the interior. So I mean to take a camel with a harem tent, and hide myself inside it until I shall have passed the Turkish guards at the gate of the town.

It is a strange sight to watch the arrival of a caravan from a distance. It resembles a long snake, growing ever bigger and bigger as it draws near. It always proceeds in the same order: first, the camels with huge packs of wool or esparto on each side of their backs; then a cavalcade of little, thin, wiry donkeys, scarcely bigger than large Newfoundland dogs, also very heavily laden, and having sometimes a stout man perched on their backs in addition to their own weight in merchandise; then crowds of men on foot, carrying nothing but long guns slung across their shoulders; and, lastly, a herd of half-ragged women, groaning under prodigious weights, and carrying their children in a kind of sack upon their backs. The whole caravan suggests a procession of phantoms, and you wonder whether you may not be face to face with some strange dream.

The most admired camels are the so-called white ones, in reality of a dingy cream colour. These are

CAMEL CAVALCADE ON THE MARCH.

also said to be the most intelligent. A camel's age may be told by his teeth with certainty up to eight years or even twelve. From fifteen to twenty he is old and well past his prime. When old and tough, he is often killed and eaten, just as a horse is in France. Distinguished travellers in the interior of North Africa are often regaled with a young camel roasted whole, but this is rather welcome for the idea of the thing than for the flavour, though the hump is generally considered a delicacy. Among camels, however, it is supposed to be an imperfection, for there is a proverb: "The camel sees not his own hump, but sees that of his brother."

Locusts. When the locust season is due, telegraphic warning of the plague's advent may be expected any day. Very few precautions are taken against the full-grown insects, who will shortly approach from the West. Indeed, in these hard times they are almost welcome as an article of food. They are deadened with oil and dried on the roofs of the houses, after which they are considered a delicacy equal, if not superior, to shrimp sauce. Forced labour is used to destroy their nests, wherever they may be found; and one result of this is, that the Arabs hesitate to notify discoveries of tainted areas, lest they may be told off to deal with them. It is doubtful, moreover, whether any amount of energy is sufficient to cope with locusts adequately. When the eggs are hatched, dense columns of wingless insects proceed in every direction, devouring every green thing and penetrating even into the houses of the villages. Corn and the leaves of olive trees they destroy utterly, palm branches they spoil severely, and even the heads of esparto-grass they attempt to damage, despite difficulties of digestion. The Cypriot net is now largely used as a prophylactic. It is some two feet high and provided with a glazed surface near the ground; but the general opinion is that it is of very little use as a barrier, unless natives are employed to tap it constantly. Greater reliance is, perhaps, placed on the aboriginal plan of luring the insects into pits, and then drowning them or trampling them to death. So far, the natives have been fairly successful in keeping them out of the chief oases, but the general attitude towards them is the patience of the fatalist, and the hope that they may soon grow wings and fly off to devastate other lands to the East.

Dogs. An Arab said to a friend of mine: "There are three things which we do not understand in Christians, and find it difficult to forgive them: they let their women go about unveiled; they eat pig; and, most horrible of all, they embrace their dogs." Muhammadans are always kind to animals—except, perhaps, to pigs they may find wandering about in their grave-yards—but they consider a dog to be an unclean animal, and elaborate ablutions are necessary after touching one. I have not been able to ascertain whether there were ever street-dogs in Tunis, as there are at Constantinople. There have certainly not been any recently, for every native I have consulted has been astonished at the very idea. In the villages of Tunisia there are plenty of dogs, who are friendly to the inhabitants but ferocious towards strangers. They are, however, more or less attached to the various households, and have not the high degree of intelligence which is developed among dogs who have to fend for themselves.

Flamingoes. The view over the lake of Tunis is often enhanced by lovely salmon-pink patches, which glitter in the sunlight. These are vast regiments of flamingoes, which the natives consider to be among the most intelligent of the lower animals. Stuffed specimens may be purchased in Tunis, but the bird requires great skill and patience to stalk. You may see thousands huddled together as they fish upon the lake; but directly you attempt to come near them, a sentinel, posted on the outskirts, gives the alarm, and the whole army makes off like a fiery flash. Naturalists, who have studied their habits, describe all sorts of evolutions, exceeding in precision and ingenuity even those of rooks or grenadiers. They have parliaments upon the water and elaborate police regulations, criminal trials (doubtless by jury), and summary executions. But, as might be expected in red-coats, their chief delight lies in military exercises. They wheel in line, march in single file, and charge at the double, under the direction of experienced sergeants and centurions—and, no doubt, if it were only possible to come a little closer to observe them, many other interesting details of military organization would be revealed.

Serpents.   There are only two dangerous kinds of snakes in Tunisia—the little horned adder, which may be easily trodden upon in the woods, and a large puff adder, which sits up and inflates itself before darting. If proper precautions be taken at once, it is possible to recover from their bites, but the poison will produce a long period of prostration. It is the large puff adder which the serpent-charmers generally display, but they sometimes take advantage of the ignorance of the crowd to produce a perfectly harmless snake of alarming size. A friend of mine was engaged upon some excavations in the interior, and had stretched his arm some way down a hole in a ruin, when he heard loud exclamations from the Arabs who were with him, and, starting back, he found that he had disturbed a huge snake, which was proceeding to coil itself round his arm. It belonged, however, to a harmless variety, and he had no difficulty in shaking it off.

Scorpions.   When the weather grows hot, it is almost impossible to go anywhere among loose stones without encountering scorpions. They have even been known to adventure themselves into houses, and it is always an useful precaution in the interior to look inside your bed and your boots to make sure that they have not ensconced themselves there. They are livid reptiles of a peculiarly revolting appearance, but as a rule their bite, though by no means pleasant, is not more dangerous than the sting of a wasp. People have, however, been known to die from the effects. A friend of mine, who was bitten, told me that the effect was an extraordinary chilling of the blood.

A certain officer vowed that he had no fear of scorpions in his boots. If ever he found one there, he would stamp it to death with his iron heel. One day he put on his top boot and felt a sting. He stamped violently, but the sting only grew sharper. He went on stamping until his patience was exhausted and his boot was full of blood. Then he took it off, and found that a practical joker had placed a spur there.

Gazelles. In Tunis itself a gazelle is by no means easy to obtain, for it has to be brought a long way from the south of the Regency, and does not always stand the rough-and-ready means of transport. When I came to Gabes, I was delighted to find a couple of gazelles gambolling in the courtyard of the little inn, and I soon made friends with them; though they never acquired anything like the tameness which my own gazelle has developed in England. One of them was a female about a year old, with long, curved horns, and the other a male of about three months, with horns which had not yet grown longer than an inch. The male was the tamer of the two, but neither of them had much confidence in strangers on first acquaintance. They seemed devoted to the landlady, who had brought them up from infancy, and they condescended to tolerate a negro servant chiefly, I fancy, on account of the excellent accent with which he imitated their bleat. They were allowed to run about the streets whenever they liked, but they never strayed very far, lest the Arab boys should be tempted to tease them. Their chief occupation was to bask in the sunshine of the courtyard, or nibble at a great bunch of Lucerne grass, hung up for their benefit, or wander into the guests' bedrooms and play with anything that took their fancy there. Nothing could exceed their mischief, and the landlady told me that one of them had bitten a huge hole in a sheet which she had hung up to air. One morning, when I was dressing, the younger gazelle stole in and carried off one of my most necessary garments into the courtyard. He stood behind a pillar with it in his mouth, surveying me with the most mischievous expression, and dodging me behind the pillars, to the intense amusement of the negro, when I attempted a pursuit. One evening their mistress had been feeding them and putting her fingers into their mouths to play with them. "Look," she remarked, "how gentle they are! They would never dream of biting me." She had scarcely said this when she gave a loud squeal, and drew away a finger from which the blood was streaming copiously. I could not help laughing, although she had evidently been severely bitten. "Poor little fellow!" she said. "It was all my own fault; for, of course, he thought I was giving him something to eat." As a matter of fact, however, a gazelle will never touch meat.

The animals evidently possessed such a keen sense of humour, and their practical jokes were always so witty, that I entreated the landlady to procure me a gazelle as soon as possible. She expressed her doubts about my being able to get it home safely to England, or to keep it alive in our arctic climate; but she mentioned that she had obtained a pair some years previously for a German, and that they had thriven exceedingly in his deer-park. Indeed, he had written to her recently to announce, with great delight, that they had just presented him with the dearest and fluffiest little gazelle imaginable, and that he hoped in process of time to possess quite a colony of them. Several days elapsed without my seeing my promised gazelle, and when the landlady told me that he could only be obtained by a piece of good fortune—if an Arab happened to have killed the mother, in order to sell her flesh in the market and her little ones as pets—I began to fear that no gazelle would turn up before the time arrived for my departure from the oasis. However, one morning the woman summoned me in a great state of excitement to say that she had found an Arab leading a young gazelle through the street, and had instantly waylaid him on my account. I hurried out into the courtyard, and found the sweetest and most miserable little object I have ever beheld. It seemed to consist of nothing but skin and bone, and its long spindle legs, covered with terrible sores where they had been tied together, would have given it a laughable aspect if one had not felt so sorry for it. It was held by a coarse rope round its neck, and cowered away from everybody trembling with fear. But even then its blue-black eyes were exceedingly beautiful, and it had an exquisitely impertinent expression about its little snub nose. I wanted to take possession of it at once, and thought half a crown dirt cheap; but the landlady had her own ideas about the etiquette of purchase in the East, and insisted on haggling for a long time, to the eventual saving of threepence. The poor little fellow was evidently half-starved, but it took several days before we could accustom him to take warm goat's milk out of a baby's bottle. He was, however, by no means stupid in learning what was expected of him, and soon developed into the sweetest little round ball of fluff, perched at the top of four ridiculous stilts, with glossy patent-leather shoes at the end of them. The other gazelles viewed him with suspicion and butted him away whenever he was inclined to make any advances to them; so he soon came to look upon us as his only friends and natural protectors.

I expected that he would prove a great trial on the long journey back to England, but he turned out exceedingly docile and accommodating. Happily, the captain and stewards on board the boats took a great fancy to him, and spared no trouble about sending ashore to fetch his daily half-litre of milk. When it was smooth, he used to frolic about the saloon and deck with exuberance, but he was always ready to be packed away again in his hamper and sleep profoundly at a moment's notice. Off the coast of Sicily I had some alarm about him, as I had been unable to obtain fresh milk and had been beguiled by his piteous appeals into giving him a dose of

condensed milk, which disagreed with him at once.
By this time I had grown so fond of him and his
pretty little ways, that I could not bear the thought
of the possibility of losing him. However, after
several bottlefuls of real milk he rapidly recovered.
I had been told that he would probably prove a
very bad sailor, but this turned out to be quite a
mistake. When the sea was roughest, and I was
feeling most anxious to remain undisturbed, he would
poke his nose into my hand and jump about, expecting me to join him in a game of play. From
Naples—where he proved far and away the most
popular person in my hotel—I travelled straight
through to England, solely on his account; and he
accommodated himself to the railway as easily as
he had done to the steamer. As the officials were
quite unaccustomed to a gazelle as a passenger, they
were puzzled to know how he ought to be treated.
In one case only—for the first stretch in Italy, and
that chiefly, I think, on account of the officiousness
of my hotel porter—I had to take a ticket for the
gazelle. The rest of the way he was as free as an
infant in arms, and, I may add, a great deal less
troublesome. Never was there so patient an animal.
If he had to go without food for a long time, or to
be stuffed into his basket when he would have liked
to play or take the air, he never emitted more than
the feeblest little bleat of protest. The man who
made out his ticket had no idea what he was.
Dogs he knew, and goats he knew, but what was
this? "A gazelle," I said.—"What is that? Is it

a monkey or a parrot?" It is astonishing what a number of animals he has been mistaken for in the course of his career. A man in Rome was heard explaining to another that he was a kangaroo, and in France every one said he was a *biche*. But perhaps his strangest experience was when he landed in England, and I had to pass him off as a basket of strawberries. The English custom-house officials were the only ones who made any objection to him anywhere during his journey. I had scarcely come off the boat, when an individual came up and asked me whether I had a licence to import a gazelle. I said, "Licence? No. Why should I want a licence? It isn't a dog." "But there is a rule that no ruminating animal may be imported without a special permit from the Board of Agriculture. You will have to telegraph for a permit, and leave him here until you get it. We will take every care of him." If I had had proper presence of mind, I should have asked the man how he knew for certain that a gazelle was a ruminating animal; but he might have opened the basket to see, and I am sure the little rascal would have been contrary enough to seize that very moment for an exhibition of his powers of ruminating. As it was, I could only plead and implore. It would surely die. It would not take its bottle from anybody but us. Would the custom-house not have pity on a poor orphan? The custom-house was decidedly inclined to have pity, but unfortunately regretted that the regulations were absolute, and it was as much as any

one's place was worth to infringe it. At last a
happy thought occurred to me, and I said, "How
do you know it is a gazelle? You have not seen
it." "No, but somebody must have done so";
and the man looked round inquiringly to his col-
leagues, who confessed that none of them had seen
it. "So," I said triumphantly, "if I tell you it is
a basket of strawberries, you will let it through."
"Well," said the man, with a grin, "if you can tell
me that it is a basket of strawberries, I shall have
no choice but to let you take it away." "All right,
then; I tell you he is a basket of strawberries," I
said in great delight, snatching him up as a brand
from the burning. As I passed the official at the
door of the custom-house, he said to me, with a
twinkle in his eye, "Lor, I don't believe that
ain't no basket of strorberries; I believe it's a
monkey."

Mr. Gabey spent his first English fortnight at
Brighton, soon growing so plump and well-liking
that no one who had seen him on his first appearance, with a rope round his neck, could ever have
recognised him for the same animal, and I soon
grew tired of the laudatory adjectives with which
every one assailed him. I took him every day
into the square gardens, where a dense mob of
cabmen, errand-boys, and all sorts of loafers, congregated round the railings to admire his jumps,
with legs stiffly outstretched, some three feet in the
air. "'Ullo, Jimmy Longlegs!" was the general
verdict.

He has now lived five months in a London flat, and enjoys the most robust health,[1] exciting the lifelong devotion of every one who is privileged to behold him. Never was anything more useful as a topic of conversation, and the narrative of his endless caprices varies every day. He has the strongest likes and dislikes, quite irrespective of any kindness which may be shown him. Indeed, he has a decided contempt for people who grovel too much to him. His aristocratic instincts inspire in him a great dislike to all menials, and he always tries to chase out of the room any one who enters it wearing a white apron. He emits loud bleats, which are almost savage, and butts at his enemy full tilt with vehemence—which will doubtless cause pain when his horns shall be full-grown. One of his favourite games is to come behind a very solemn parlourmaid, and suddenly tug at the streamers of her cap when she is most rigidly upon her dignity. If I hold a napkin in front of me and pretend that it is an apron, he is visibly disturbed, and grunts his disapproval, though he knows who it is all the time. On the other hand, he has a great partiality for black clothes, probably because he was first fed with a bottle held against a black skirt. This black skirt he has by no means forgotten, and if he sees it hanging up anywhere, he rushes up to paw it and ask it for

---

[1] Alas, since writing the above, my poor Gabey has succumbed to the abominable climate of Wales. The subject is, however, too painful to enlarge upon. I miss him more than I should miss any human child. Inshallah; may his soul rest in peace!

food. Then when it takes no notice of him, he proceeds to punish it by biting large holes in it.

His taste in food is of infinite variety. What he likes best of all is a cigarette end or a spoonful of apricot jam. He also considers a wax match a great delicacy, but that is not often allowed him lest he should develop an attack of phossy-jaw. He likes fruit of nearly every kind and would be delightfully destructive in a garden. If you give him a cherry he proceeds to play at the bobbing game before eating it. He takes the end of the stalk in his mouth, draws the fruit up with great patience in the most comical manner, and has never yet been caught cheating. Strawberry stalks and stewed fruit, with a great deal of sugar, are always welcome to him, but he is generally ready to eat up a whole spoonful of salt, which he finds useful as an appetiser. For some days he raved about lump sugar and would do almost anything to obtain it, but now he has taken a sudden distaste to it, and turns away with a sniff when it is offered. He has a great curiosity about new forms of food, and when I am at breakfast he thinks it a great joke to creep up suddenly behind me and stuff his nose into my plate, or both forelegs into my tea-cup. If there is a great upset, he is greatly amused, and trots about the room with his head in the air, convinced he has done something exceedingly clever. He never neglects an opportunity of gnawing a piece of paper. If it is very thin, it soon disappears down his throat, but, if it is thick, he only plays with it as a dog with a bone.

More than once I have left a pile of letters within his reach, and when I have returned he has greeted me with every possible expression of merriment, and I have found several of the letters reduced to a pulp. If he is dull, he can always occupy himself with a newspaper; when the cover is not to his taste he tears it off, then he turns over the pages and sniffs them just as if he were engaged in mastering their contents. I regret to say that he has a decided preference for light literature, such as the *Sporting Times* and the theatrical columns of the *Sketch*. This accounts for the fact that he always thinks in the very latest slang, as you may see by watching his expression when he walks about the room carrying a straw in his mouth like a groom. Another of his diversions is to go under the table at meal times and quietly bite all your bootlaces in two. He will often leave them hanging by a thread, so that when you get into the street, they will all burst simultaneously. He will also lick all the blacking off, so that your boots appear as if you have been walking through a river. He is never so happy as when he can creep into a dressing room where a number of boots are laid out. Then he sits himself solemnly down and spends the whole afternoon in making a meal off them. I am sure he must have some Semitic blood in his veins, for he delights in anything bright, particularly gold, silver, and jewellery, which he will gnaw by the hour whenever he is permitted to do so. He will chew up a pearl button in no time, and if a pin, needle, hook or eye is left about on the carpet, he never fails to appropriate it. I am always afraid that his rashness in this respect may bring him to an untimely end. It is certainly far more dangerous to him than the English climate, which, after all, is not much more trying than that of some parts of Tunisia. As he is an Arab, I suppose one ought also to fear for him the dangers of the evil eye, and I always shudder whenever any one tries to show off his knowledge by quoting Tom Moore's unfortunately familiar lines about the "dear Gazelle." Certain it is that, when the other day a foolish woman of my acquaintance had exclaimed, "What an idea to have a gazelle, I am sure I hope it will die," he suddenly took to refusing his food, and showed signs of pining away. When, however, I had hung a potent amulet round his neck, the spell was immediately broken, and his appetite and sturdiness revived.

He is one of the best companions I know, and will keep up a conversation for a long time, answering every remark with the most expressive bleats and grunts, as if he understood precisely what was said to him. When he is affectionately disposed, he puts up his nose and sniffs my face with great diligence. This is his idea of kissing. He cannot bear to be left alone for an instant, and directly I get up to leave a room he makes a point of trotting out after me. However sleepy he may be in the evening, he is always reluctant from being taken off to his rug in the scullery; and directly he is let out in the morning he rushes off and scratches at my bedroom door, imploring admission. As he has taken so extremely well to his life in England, and is doted on by every one who sees him, I can only wonder how it is that people in England do not more often import gazelles as pets. No doubt they require a great deal of patience, but their many charms afford an ample reward for its expenditure.

Chapter XI

TRIPOLI

The Town—The Outskirts—Security—Commerce—Palm-wine—
The Future of Tripoli.

The Town. FIRST impressions of Tripoli are undoubtedly the best. Beheld from the steamer, across a dazzling sea of every shade of blue, her white sheen and graceful outlines are a bountiful delight. At either end of the curving bay are sturdy forts: on one side the Kasr or Citadel, on the other the Spanish and the Bordj-el-lilla, or One Night Fort, said to have been built by the Jinns in that short space of time. Between these extremities is the venerable wall which encircles the whole town and must have rendered it well-nigh impregnable in the days before artillery. The town itself seems a strange collection of huddled houses with flat roofs straggling up the hill, mosque domes, and rounded minarets, which strike a contrast after the square turret shapes of Tunisia, and on all hands are visions of verdant gardens with projecting palms. The Customs' formalities are very slow: your passport is taken away, your name and profession are noted down in Turkish characters, and if you confess to no profession, you are gravely inscribed as a "Milor." Inside the walls the town belies expectations, though it is not without certain charms of its own. The streets are so narrow that you may drive but a part of the way to your destination, and they are paved with such primæval boulders that all transit is a torture. The only vehicles obtainable are a kind of springless governess cart, of brightly-painted wood, provided with an armoury of coloured awnings against the raging sun. They are infinitely picturesque, but even less comfortable than an Irish jaunting-car. The driver crouches on the shaft, while the fares hug the seats and woodwork in wild endeavours to keep themselves and their belongings from being flung on to the floor or the road. I know of no more infallible recipe for a headache than half an hour's torture in such a conveyance amid the constant dust and glare. At each of the town gates a stone obstacle, more than a foot high, stretches right across the way and is negotiated at a brisk trot with consequences which are painful to remember. The houses have either an ugly modern frontage or are tumble-down hovels reeking with the refuse of generations, but nearly every street is covered in with ragged matting and an abundance of verdure which afford a picturesque atonement for every outrage. There is by no means the same variety of costume as that which glorifies the greater part of Tunisia. Turks wear the fez with a kind of frock coat, and most of the Arabs restrict themselves to a monotonous white or drab coat, called a *barracan*, which covers the whole body from head to foot. But on hey-days the Jewesses wear long full trousers and zouaves, which are far richer and more graceful than those in any other part of Barbary. The inns are as bad as any in the Levant, and even the least fastidious traveller will hesitate to spend a week in them between the boats. Nor are there any sights to tempt him. He may not enter the mosques, and the famous Roman arch of white marble, reported not long ago to be the finest in existence, is now half buried in rubbish heaps and walled up for use as a Maltese grog-shop. And yet there are about Tripoli a quiet charm which it is impossible to explain or define, many unique characteristics appertaining to the last Turkish stronghold in Africa, and much food for interesting reflection by the roving politician.

The Outskirts. Tawdry modern suburbs are in process of erection, but a ride outside Tripoli is still a delight. The oasis is a series of luxurious gardens, protected by high mud walls against possible marauders, and the warm air is laden with the perfume of lemon-blossom. The profusion of oranges supplies most of the markets of the world, and nearly all those which are known to the trade as Malta bloods are exported hence. Mulberries and apricots are ripe at the end of April, and Japanese medlars, picked with the sun on them, are peculiarly luscious. The fringe of the desert is but a few yards away and, unlike the various deserts in North Tunisia, presents the traditional expanse of bright yellow sand, stretching away as far as the eye can reach without ever a trace of vegetation. Further along the oasis is a negro village, whither it is the fashion to repair and witness strange barbaric dances by the light of a full moon. The huts are of true tropical appearance, strange erections of mud and leaves, with porches of bamboo palisade. Travellers may wander in the near vicinity of Tripoli where they will, but journeying in the interior is discouraged, chiefly because the Government cannot hold themselves responsible for security at a distance from towns, but partly also because the present Pasha is a strict Moslem and disinclined to afford facilities to inquisitive infidels. He is somewhat of a fanatic, and has been seen to embrace Dervishes and mad Merabuts in the public streets. There is, however, nothing to warrant a desire to explore the interior of the Vilayet. Beyond a few hares and red-legged partridges there is no pretext for the sportsman, and theories of archæological treasures are probably unfounded. An Englishman, who contrived to elude the authorities a couple of years ago, claims to have found trilithons, indicative of Baal worship, in the neighbouring hill-ranges, but residents at Gabes aver that similar models are employed for oil-mills there to this day.

Security. One of the most striking features of Tripoli is the ubiquity of soldiers and barracks. The barracks are airy, cheerful buildings, provided in every case with pleasant gardens. The soldiers are sturdy, good-natured youths, who lounge about the streets hand-in-hand. Their uniforms are of thick, dark frieze, patched and darned and ragged beyond description. There are also plenty of policemen in the town, and any symptom of disorder would be speedily repressed. But the Arab

population is of a gentle and law-abiding disposition.
Indeed, every face I saw seemed to beam a welcome.
Under a clump of palm trees at the entrance to the
desert I entered into conversation with a party of
Beduins, who were resting their camels before em-
barking on the sands. They answered every enquiry
with ready courtesy, and I had the utmost difficulty in
excusing myself from accepting their invitation to
"come and eat mutton" with them. When I expressed a wish to see a garden in the oasis, the proprietor received me with open arms, and insisted on
loading me with fruit and lemon-blossoms. The only
source for serious anxiety in Tripoli is the strong distaste for military service under the Turks. This
led to disturbances in the neighbouring villages in
1898, and may do so again. In the town itself an
European may wander about at any time of the day
or night as safely as in any other capital. It is true
that the Jews do not venture outside their quarters
after dark, but they always err on the side of excessive
caution, and it is significant that there have been no
anti-Semitic disturbances in Tripoli as in Tunis and
Algeria.

Commerce. As the French have not yet succeeded in re-establishing caravans between Tunisia and the interior, Tripoli now commands a monopoly in this part of North Africa. This is mainly due to the maintenance of the Turkish garrison at Khadames, a town so fanatical that no Christian is permitted to enter it. Most of the ostrich feathers of the interior are brought to Tripoli, and fine specimens may, with perseverance, be purchased in the bazaars. Quaint Sudanese garments, saddlery, arrows and other weapons, horns, skins, and curiosities may also be picked up, but the shops are not so tempting as might be expected, and the merchants, who are nearly all Jews, ask extravagant prices. The native carpets are now by no means what they were, aniline dyes having come into use and the work being less thoroughly done. Of course there is still a considerable export of esparto. Trade with Tunisia has suffered from the imposition of the maximum tariff against imports by sea from Tripoli, but Free Trade practically exists by land. The Turks, who still regard Tunisia as a Turkish province, apply their regulation of free trade between one province and another by land, while the French do not consider that the receipts would counterbalance the expenditure of establishing customhouses on the long and ill-defined frontier of Tripoli; but they reserve their right to seize and tax any large consignments which may have evaded duty in this way.

Palm-wine. A great deal of *lagmi*, or palm-wine, is consumed at Tripoli. The extraction of it generally kills a palm tree, which has a market value of five pounds, and there is a tax of one pound on each tree killed in this way. As it is still worth while to go through with the operation, some idea may be formed of the quantity of sap obtained for sale at a halfpenny the pint. The *lagmi* is sweet and fresh in the morning immediately after it has been drawn, but by night time it has been turned into a fermented beverage, slightly effervescing and agreeable to the taste. Yeast is often added to promote the fermentation. Every consumer of *lagni* has his own opinions as to the best time for drinking the beverage. Most people prefer it either fresh from the tree or else after it has been fermented, and consider it excessively nasty at the various stages in between.

The Future of Tripoli. The importance of Tripoli does not seem to be fully appreciated by British statesmen; and it is well to utter a word of warning, lest it should one day share the fate of Tunis. It is true that the coast-line, though equal in length to that of Tunisia and Algeria, is for the most part arid and desolate; but we must not forget that the town is, and is likely to remain, the principal commercial avenue from the Barbary states to the interior, where so many rival interests are at stake. There is, of course, no sign that Turkey will be called upon to part with it in our time, but it were surely well to be prepared. Should the Arabs' distaste for Turkish military service lead to a general rising, the French might not be above proclaiming themselves protectors of the Arab race in Africa. The Italians, too, undeterred by their unbroken series of reverses, still cherish an aspiration to the reversion of Tripoli. It is to foster this that they subsidize the Florio-Rubattino service of steamers, which is exceedingly agreeable to the few passengers who avail themselves of it, but must cost a pretty penny. Should the occasion arise, it may be useful to remind both France and Italy that Tripoli was formerly a dependency of Malta.

INDEX

Abuse, 89-90, 124
Acreage, 264
Agriculture, 28, 29, 39, 218, 263-268
Ahmed Bey, 10
Aïssawas, 106-109, 203
Alawi College, 294
Algeria, 31, 32, 39, 42, 77, 96, 121, 122, 259
Ali, Bey of Tunis, 11-24, 27, 32, 105, 276, 279, 280
Aqueduct, Bardo, 5
Amphitheatres, 112, 210-211, 216, 223, 226
Amulets, 53, 110, 112-114, 141, 176, 216, 217, 325
Angels, Guardian, 133
Antisemites, 37, 122-124, 131, 331
Arab administration, 28, 293
Arabesques, 49, 66, 68, 69
Arabs, 7, 8, 46-91, 216, 227, 269, 330-331
Arabs and French, 35, 42, 225, 286-287, 290-292, 333
Arabs and Jews, 123-124
Archæology, 2, 63, 175, 176, 216, 223, 226, 228, 229, 330
Arms, 254, 257
Army, 30
Arrival in Tunis, 144-146
Art, Arab, 74, 188, 189, 190, 291

Baghdad, *Meraïout* of, 109-110
Bairam, 13, 15, 98, 99-105
Bankruptcy, 121
Bazaars, 119, 151, 236-245, 249, 251, 254-257
Beds and bedrooms, 49, 67, 68, 73, 129
Bees, 218
Beggars, 87, 166, 169
Beja, 193, 226-227
Benghazi, 259, 260
Berbers, 1, 7, 8, 222
Berlin Congress, 10, 43
Beys, 9, 10, 11-24, 27, 29, 123, 220, 265, 289
Bicycles, 189, 190
Birds, 73, 227
Bizerta, 48, 80, 193, 213, 229-235, 269
Blood-money, 272, 276, 279, 280, 283
Bodyguard of the Bey, 16, 30
Bukhra, 133, 137, 141
Buonaparte, N., 9
Butchers, 119, 130, 132, 151, 203
Byzantines, 7, 8, 227

Cabs, 328
Cactus, 266, 296

Camels, 19, 59, 101, 161, 186-187, 189, 203, 216, 264, 266, 295-311
Canal, Tunis, 144
Capital punishment, 283-284 (see also Executions)
Capitulations, 273
Caravans, 187, 222, 258-261, 263, 308, 331
Carpets, 59, 238, 248, 253-254, 261
Carthage, 2, 3, 7, 137, 167, 169, 170-183, 288
Carthaginians, 1-3, 63, 226, 227
Charles the Great, 8
Charles V., 9
Children, 55, 68, 76, 103-104, 106, 169
Church, Anglican, 165-166
Cisterns, 171, 173, 179, 226
Civil list, 13, 28
Clocks, 23, 69
Coburg, Duchess of, 72
Colleges, 289-294
Colonization, 39, 40, 42, 50
Commerce, 30, 40, 43, 236-245, 254-257, 258-262, 331-332
Communications, 37, 38 (see also Railways)
Conscription, 30
Contrôleurs civils, 27, 28, 34, 204, 220, 273
Corvée, see Forced labour
Costumes, 48-49, 52, 57, 67, 74, 101-102, 123, 134, 140, 141, 143, 146-148, 151, 188, 197-198, 212, 213, 222, 328
Cottons, 44, 261
Crapaudine, 30
Crémieux, 32

Custom-houses, 40, 41, 145, 259, 320-321, 327, 332

DANCES, 98, 99, 100, 101, 142, 329
Dido, 2, 183
Diligences, 37, 38
Divorce, 79-80
Dogs, 33, 49, 59, 287, 312
Doors, 66, 110, 111, 153
Dowries, 78
Drugs, 48, 66, 78, 84, 139
Drunkenness, 105
Dugga, 193, 227-229
Dwellings, 49, 50, 51, 58, 60-63, 66-74, 129, 215, 328, 330
Dwirat, 62, 193
Dyeing, 247

EDUCATION, 28, 120, 287-294
El-Jem, 38, 112, 193, 210-211, 216
El-Kef, 193, 225-226
England's lost opportunity, 42-45
Enzels, 265, 267, 292
Esparto, see Halfa-grass
Evil-eye, 66, 68, 69, 78, 110, 112, 140, 244, 325
Excavations, 2, 175
Executions, public, 275-281, 283
Exports, 1, 29, 30

FAMILY, the Jewish, 137-139
Fantasias, 188
Fatalism, 148, 281, 312
Feriana, 193
Ferry, 232, 233
Finance, 10, 28-29, 125
Fishing, 193, 213, 230, 268-271
Flamingoes, 145, 313
Flies, 129, 151, 203

INDEX

Flowers, 78, 194, 209, 210, 213
Fonduks, 186-187, 299
Food, 67, 73, 79, 81-83, 137, 141, 165
Forced labour, 29, 311
Fortifications, 213-214, 221, 230, 231
Fortune tellers, 114-117
French administration, 4, 11, 12, 27-45, 284-287
French aggression, 10, 95, 287, 333
French concession to crime, 283
French craft, 11, 32, 33, 230, 260
French distractions, 157, 204
French exactions, 4, 29, 34-35, 41, 44, 259, 289
French failures and shortcomings, 37, 39, 42, 121, 122, 179, 259, 260, 263, 267, 268, 273
French impede research and travel, 2, 35-36, 38, 186, 223
French improvement, 267
French quarter of Tunis, 126, 157-162
French rudeness, 14, 146, 185, 224-225, 293
French servants, 165
French spy-mania, 36, 234
French tyranny, 4, 30-31, 32, 36, 37, 224-225
French unpopularity, 35, 120, 262
French vulgarize and demoralize natives, 74, 104, 184, 247, 290-292
Fruit, 104, 151, 161, 165, 266, 329
Funerals, 80, 142, 233
Furniture, 69, 73, 129
Future of Tripoli, 333

Future of Tunisia, 42

GABES, 34, 40, 59, 121, 185, 193, 214-219, 254, 260, 330
Gafsa, 59, 186, 193
Gardens, 16, 30, 41, 58, 211, 215, 218, 254, 331
Gazelles, 19, 66, 91, 315-326
Genseric, 4, 7
Governor of Tunis, 274-275
Graveyards, 95-97, *see also* Tombs
Greeks, 39, 213, 269, 270, 271
Greetings, 88-89
Guilds, 243
Gurbis, 50, 51, 52, 197

HABEUS, 32, 265, 267, 292
Halfa-grass, 257-258, 300, 311, 332
Hammamet, 193
Hannibal, 2, 183
Harbours, 230, 234
Harems, 64, 74
Hashish, 84-85
Hemp, 84, 151
Heretics, Moslem, 221
Hinterlands, Mediterranean, 260-261
History, 1-10
Hotels, 162, 165, 185-186, 233, 234, 329
Houses, *see Dwellings*
Housetops, 49
Humt Suk, 219, 220, 221
Hussein, 9

IMAGINATION, 78, 104
Incense, 96
Industries, 30, 51, 58, 119, 120, 222, 243, 244, 247, 248, 253, 254, 257, 258

Inhabitants, original, 1
Interior of Africa, 258-263
Interior of Tunisia, 33, 37, 50-64, 184-235, 311
Invocation of Saints, 97
Ironmongers, 120
Irrigation, 59, 217
Islam, 92-117, 137, 209, 290
Italians, 39, 42, 170, 269, 271, 283-284
Itinerary, an, 190, 193

JAMA'AL, 243
Janissaries, 9
Jem, El, *see El-Jem*
Jerba Island, 193, 219-222, 247, 254, 257, 270
Jews, 28, 32, 35, 90, 100, 101, 118-126, 129-143, 217, 273, 289, 328, 331
Jews, Leghorn, 118
Jewellery, 48, 52, 53, 67
Jinns, 63, 68, 87, 107, 110-111, 133, 152
Justice, 109, 125-126, 138, 272-274, 275-287
Justinian, 7

KADIS, 272, 273-274
Kaïds, 27, 28, 125, 224, 272
Kairwân, 7, 34, 37, 95, 106, 185, 193, 196, 197-204, 205, 207, 209, 212, 238, 240, 247, 248
Kakawia, 83
Karagus, 98
Kasserin, 193
Kef, El, *see El-Kef*
Kerkenna Islands, 193, 213, 269, 270
Khammes, 264
Khalifas, 28
Kif, 84

Kitchen, Arab, 73
Koran, 59, 77, 96, 106, 272, 294
Krumirs, 10, 50

LAKES, 179, 193, 230, 232, 269
Land, 218, 263-265 (*see also Habbus*)
Language, 63, 86-88, 216, 222
Lavigerie, Cardinal, 136, 170, 175, 288
Laws, 32, 125
Locusts, 81, 311-312
Louis, Saint, 170, 179, 180
Lybian language, 229

MAHDIA, 269
Maktar, 193
Maltese, 39, 42, 48, 221, 333
Marionettes, 101
Markets, 203, 212, 227
Marriage, Arab, 64, 65, 76-79
Marriage, Jewish, 138, 139-142
Marsa, 12, 13, 15, 170
Massinissa, 3
Matmatas, 60, 61, 193
Medecine, 74, 86
Mednin, 62, 121, 193
Mejba, 29
Mejerda, 50, 193, 227
Menagery, 19
Merabuts, 96, 109, 110, 204, 227, 244, 330
Merchants, 87, 236, 237, 239, 243, 332
Milk, 136
Millet, M., *see Resident*
Ministers of the Bey, 27
Missionaries, 35-36, 75, 136-137, 175, 216
Mogods, 193

INDEX

Mosaics, 111, 229
Mosques, 94, 95, 98, 122, 198, 201, 203, 221, 226, 281, 287, 294, 329
Motor-cars, 190
Mrharsa, 264
Museum, 176
Music, 98, 101, 142
Mustahal, 80

NABEUL, 193, 254-257
Naturalization, 35
Nefta, 193
Negroes, 66, 73, 113, 114, 115, 143, 329

OASES, 54-59, 254, 261, 312, 329 (*see also Gabes*)
Oil, 82, 268
Olives, 30, 267-268, 311
Order of the Blood, 14

PAGANISM, 221, 330
Palaces of the Bey, 11, 12, 13, 15-24, 276
Patriarchal system, 63-64
Palms, 30, 216
Palm-wine, 83, 332
Passports, 36-37, 285
Penal laws against Jews, 123-124
Peplos, 52-57
Phœnicians, 1
Photography, 94, 105-106
Phylloxera, 266
Playfair, Sir L., 36
Ploughing, 264
Police, 36, 105, 284-286, 330
Poll-tax, *see Mejba*
Polygamy, 137
Poor-laws, Jewish, 125
Population, 264

Ports of Carthage, 179
Post Office, 28
Pottery, 51, 222, 257
Press laws, 36, 37
Priests, Muhammadan, 93
Prisons, 281
Proverbs, 77, 90-91, 311
Pulps, 271

RABBIS, 119, 130, 132, 137
Railways, 37, 170, 193-197, 226, 232, 260
Ramadan, 97-99, 105
Religion, Jewish, 130-137
Religion, Muhammadan, *see Islam*
Rents, 30
Resident, French, 12, 13, 14, 15, 27, 32
Revenge, Arab, 282
Révoil, M., 27
Rhadames, 222, 259, 260, 261-262, 331
Rhat, 259, 261, 262
Rhumeracen, 62
Ritual, Jewish, 131-132
Romans, 2, 3, 4, 5, 8, 63, 176, 180, 183, 222
Rosaries, 132, 217, 273
Russians, 230

SABBATH, Jewish, 129, 134-135
Sabra, 204, 209
Saddlery, 243-245
Sadiki College, 289-293
Sahara, 258-260, 262
Saints, Jewish, 132-133
Saints, Muhammadan, *see Merabuts*
Salisbury, Lord, 10, 43, 44
Sanctuary, 281-283

Sandstorm, 218-219
Sbeitla, 193, 222-223
Schools, 287-289
Scipios, 2, 3
Scorpions, 314-315
Seats, 66, 67
Security, 33, 34, 37, 64-65, 198, 280, 330-331
Sers, 50
Servants, 64, 69, 70, 71, 74, 165
Sfax, 36, 38, 95, 185, 193, 211-214, 247, 254, 271
Sheep, Sahara, 19
Sheikhs, 28, 104, 108
Sheshias, 14, 48, 53, 247, 261
Shnini, 60, 62
Shops, 119, 129, 151-152, 188, 214, 254, 255 (*see also Bazaars*)
Shrines, 109
Sidi Bu Saïd, 163, 170
Siliana, 50
Silks, 254, 261
Skulls, Tower of, 220
Slaves, 64, 65, 77, 243, 264
Slippers, 48, 54, 67, 78, 96, 102, 138, 139, 147
Snake-charmers, 112, 152, 155, 157
Snakes, 217, 314
Spaniards, 50, 221, 231
Sponges, 269-271
Steamers, 37, 193, 214
Story-tellers, 98, 152
Streets, 126, 147, 148-151, 158, 162, 199, 207, 212, 216, 243, 328
Susa, 37, 38, 185, 187, 189, 192, 193, 194, 197, 209, 212, 247, 254
Swassi, 166, 254
Synagogues, 130-131

Taïb Bey, 15
Tailors, 119
Tanning, 247-248
Tatawin, 62, 193, 261
Tattooing, 216
Taxation, 9, 29-30, 125
Tea, 83
Tebursuk, 193, 227
Temples, 223, 226, 229
Thala, 193, 223-225
Theatres, 157
Tides, 221, 269
Tiles, 49, 66, 68, 198, 257
Tobacco, 84
Tombs, 176, 177, 179, 227, 244
Torture, 30 31
Touts, 236-238
Tozer, 193
Tramways, 37-38, 161, 194, 197, 203
Treaty, Commercial, 43-45
Tribunals, 125, 126, 272
Tripoli, 41, 42, 259, 260, 261, 270, 308, 327-333
Troglodytes, 60-63
Tuaregs, 63, 71, 259, 260, 262-3
Tunis, 11, 17, 20-23, 47-50, 66, 95, 100-105, 109, 110, 118, 126, 127, 136, 143, 144-169, 180, 188, 198, 212, 218, 219, 238, 240, 247, 254, 257, 260, 269
Turks, 9, 41, 42, 260, 261, 262, 270, 328, 330, 331, 332, 333

University, Muhammadan, 294

Valensi, General, 12, 14, 16
Vandals, 4, 7, 8
Vermin, 187
Villages, 58, 210, 215, 219
Vines, 266-267

INDEX

Vivian, Mrs., 36. 59, 65-74, 81, 99, 102, 103, 117, 175, 188, 190, 194, 209, 212, 214, 215, 217, 220, 233, 274-275

WAILING, 80
Wages, 264
Water, 83, 133-134, 151-152, 265
Weight-carrying, 161
Wells, 59, 133, 217, 219, 265-266, 301
Whitewashing, 143
Wine, 266-267

Women, 48, 49, 51, 52, 53, 54, 55, 57, 58, 59, 64, 66, 69, 70, 71, 72, 73, 74, 75, 76, 89, 91, 105, 106, 134, 135, 139, 140, 148, 198, 248, 253, 264, 308
Woollens, 261
Works, public, 28

YORK, Duke of, 13

ZAGHWAN, 193, 247
Zama, 23, 193
Zarzis, 261, 269
Zawias, 122, 132

www.ingramcontent.com/pod-product-compliance
Lightning Source LLC
Chambersburg PA
CBHW030316240426
43673CB00040B/1185